Microsoft® Excel 7 for Windows® 95

Illustrated Brief Edition

Elizabeth Eisner Reding

COURSE TECHNOLOGY, INC.

A DIVISION OF COURSE TECHNOLOGY

COMMUNICATIONS GROUP

ONE MAIN STREET, CAMBRIDGE MA 02142

AN INTERNATIONAL THOMSON PUBLISHING COMPANY

I(T)P

Albany • Bonn • Boston • Cincinnati • London • Madrid • Melbourne • Mexico City
New York • Paris • San Francisco • Singapore • Tokyo • Toronto • Washington

Microsoft Excel 7 for Windows 95 — Illustrated Brief Edition is published by Course Technology, Inc.

Managing Editor:	Marjorie Hunt
Senior Product Manager:	Nicole Jones Pinard
Production Editor:	Catherine D. Griffin
Text Designer:	Leslie Hartwell
Cover Designer:	John Gamache

©1996 Course Technology, Inc.
A Division of International Thomson Publishing, Inc.

For more information contact:
Course Technology, Inc.
One Main Street
Cambridge, MA 02142

International Thomson Publishing Europe
Berkshire House 168-173
High Holborn
London WCIV 7AA
England

International Thomson Publishing GmbH
Königswinterer Strasse 418
53277 Bonn
Germany

Thomas Nelson Australia
102 Dodds Street
South Melbourne, 3205
Victoria, Australia

International Thomson Publishing Asia
211 Henderson Road
#05-10 Henderson Building
Singapore 0315

Nelson Canada
1120 Birchmount Road
Scarborough, Ontario
Canada M1K 5G4

International Thomson Publishing Japan
Hirakawacho Kyowa Building, 3F
2-2-1 Hirakawacho
Chiyoda-ku, Tokyo 102
Japan

International Thomson Editores
Campos Eliseos 385, Piso 7
Col. Polanco
11560 Mexico D.F. Mexico

Trademarks

Course Technology and the open book logo are registered trademarks of Course Technology, Inc.

I(T)P The ITP logo is a trademark under license.

Some of the product names in this book have been used for identification purposes only and may be trademarks or registered trademarks of their respective manufacturers and sellers.

Disclaimer

Course Technology, Inc. reserves the right to revise this publication and make changes from time to time in its content without notice.

0-7600-3811-2

Printed in the United States of America

10 9 8 7 6 5 4 3

From the Publisher

At Course Technology, Inc., we believe that technology will transform the way that people teach and learn. We are very excited about bringing you, instructors and students, the most practical and affordable technology-related products available.

The Course Technology Development Process

Our development process is unparalleled in the educational publishing industry. Every product we create goes through an exacting process of design, development, review, and testing.

Reviewers give us direction and insight that shape our manuscripts and bring them up to the latest standards. Every manuscript is quality tested. Students whose backgrounds match the intended audience work through every keystroke, carefully checking for clarity and pointing out errors in logic and sequence. Together with our own technical reviewers, these testers help us ensure that everything that carries our name is as error-free and easy to use as possible.

Course Technology Products

We show both how and why technology is critical to solving problems in the classroom and in whatever field you choose to teach or pursue. Our time-tested, step-by-step instructions provide unparalleled clarity. Examples and applications are chosen and crafted to motivate students.

The Course Technology Team

This book will suit your needs because it was delivered quickly, efficiently, and affordably. In every aspect of business, we rely on a commitment to quality and the use of technology. Every employee contributes to this process. The names of all our employees are listed below.
Diana Armington, Tim Ashe, Charles Baker, Sara Ballestero, Debora Barrow, Karen Bartlett, Stephen M. Bayle, Jay Bounty, Ann Marie Buconjic, Kerry Cannell, Jei Lee Chong, Jim Chrysikos, Barbara Clemens, Susan Collins, John M. Connolly, Myrna D'Addario, Jodi Davis, Howard S. Diamond, Jennifer Dolan, Joseph B. Dougherty, Patti Dowley, Laurie Duncan, Karen Dwyer, MaryJane Dwyer, Chris Elkhill, Shelley Engdahl, Don Fabricant, Ronan Fagan, Jodi Fazio, Dean Fossella, Jane Fraser, Viktor Frengut, Jeff Goding, Eileen Gorham, Chris Greacen, Catherine D. Griffin, Kathy Griffin, Jamie Harper, Roslyn Hooley, Marjorie Hunt, Matt Kenslea, Marybeth LaFauci, Susannah Lean, Chris Logan, Nancy Ludlow, Kim Mai, Margaret Makowski, Tammy Marciano, Elizabeth Martinez, Don Maynard, Kathleen McCann, Sarah McLean, Jay McNamara, Mac Mendelsohn, Karla Mitchell, Kim Munsell, Julie Neitlich, Eileen Olszewski, Michael Ormsby, Debbie Parlee, Kristin Patrick, Darren Perl, Nicole Jones Pinard, Nancy Ray, Natalie Sawin, Jana Seifert, Carla Sharpe, Roger Skilling, Christine Spillett, Alan Spira, Kristin Taggart, Audrey Tortolani, Michelle Tucker, David Upton, Jim Valente, Mark Valentine, Renee Walkup, Tracy Wells, Donna Whiting, Rob Williams, Janet Wilson, Lisa Yameen

Preface

Welcome to *Microsoft Excel 7 for Windows 95 — Illustrated Brief Edition*. This highly visual book offers new users a hands-on introduction to Microsoft Excel 7 and also serves as an excellent reference for future use. It assumes that students have learned basic Windows 95 skills and file management from *Microsoft Windows 95 — Illustrated Brief Edition* or from an equivalent book.

Organization and Coverage

Microsoft Excel 7 for Windows 95 — Illustrated Brief Edition contains four units that cover basic Excel skills. In these units students learn how to design, create, edit, and enhance Excel workbooks. They also learn how to chart their data.

Approach

Microsoft Excel 7 for Windows 95 — Illustrated Brief Edition provides new users of Excel with a highly visual and interactive learning experience. This hands-on approach makes it ideal for both self-paced or instructor-led classes.

Lessons: Information Displays

The basic lesson format of this text is the "information display," a two-page lesson that is sharply focused on a specific task. This sharp focus and the precise beginning and end of a lesson make it easy for students to study specific material. Modular lessons are less overwhelming for students, and they provide instructors with more flexibility in planning classes and assigning specific work. The units are modular as well and can be presented in any order.

Each lesson, or "information display," contains the following elements:

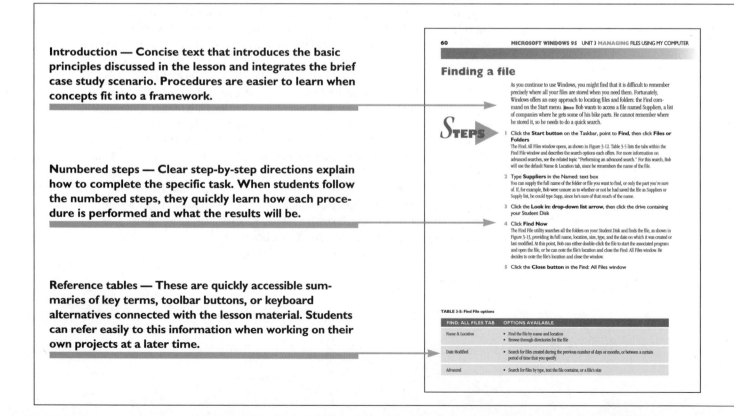

Introduction — Concise text that introduces the basic principles discussed in the lesson and integrates the brief case study scenario. Procedures are easier to learn when concepts fit into a framework.

Numbered steps — Clear step-by-step directions explain how to complete the specific task. When students follow the numbered steps, they quickly learn how each procedure is performed and what the results will be.

Reference tables — These are quickly accessible summaries of key terms, toolbar buttons, or keyboard alternatives connected with the lesson material. Students can refer easily to this information when working on their own projects at a later time.

---

60   MICROSOFT WINDOWS 95   UNIT 3 MANAGING FILES USING MY COMPUTER

Finding a file

As you continue to use Windows, you might find that it is difficult to remember precisely where all your files are stored when you need them. Fortunately, Windows offers an easy approach to locating files and folders: the Find command on the Start menu. Bob wants to access a file named Suppliers, a list of companies where he gets some of his bike parts. He cannot remember where he stored it, so he needs to do a quick search.

STEPS

1. Click the **Start button** on the Taskbar, point to **Find**, then click **Files or Folders**
   The Find: All Files window opens, as shown in Figure 3-12. Table 3-5 lists the tabs within the Find File window and describes the search options each offers. For more information on advanced searches, see the related topic "Performing an advanced search." For this search, Bob will use the default Name & Location tab, since he remembers the name of the file.

2. Type **Suppliers** in the Named: text box
   You can supply the full name of the folder or file you want to find, or only the part you're sure of. If, for example, Bob were unsure as to whether or not he had saved the file as Suppliers or Supply list, he could type Supp, since he's sure of that much of the name.

3. Click the **Look in: drop-down list arrow**, then click the drive containing your Student Disk

4. Click **Find Now**
   The Find File utility searches all the folders on your Student Disk and finds the file, as shown in Figure 3-13, providing its full name, location, size, type, and the date on which it was created or last modified. At this point, Bob can either double-click the file to start the associated program and open the file, or he can note the file's location and close the Find: All Files window. He decides to note the file's location and close the window.

5. Click the **Close button** in the Find: All Files window

TABLE 3-5: Find File options

FIND: ALL FILES TAB	OPTIONS AVAILABLE
Name & Location	• Find the file by name and location • Browse through directories for the file
Date Modified	• Search for files created during the previous number of days or months, or between a certain period of time that you specify
Advanced	• Search for files by type, text the file contains, or a file's size

Other Features

The two-page lesson format featured in this book provides the new user with a powerful learning experience. Additionally, this book contains the following features:

- "Read This Before You Begin Microsoft Excel 7" page — This page provides essential information that both students and instructors need to know before they begin working through the units.

- Real-World Case — The case used throughout the textbook is designed to be "real world" in nature and representative of the kinds of activities that students will encounter when working with Excel 7. The process of solving the problem will be more meaningful to students. A case icon identifies where the case starts in each lesson.

- End-of-Unit Material — Each unit concludes with a Task Reference that summarizes the various methods used to execute each of the skills covered in the unit. The Task Reference is followed by a meaningful Concepts Review that tests students' understanding of what they learned in the unit. The Concepts Review is followed by a Skills Review, which provides students with additional hands-on practice of the skills they learned in the unit. The Skills Review is followed by Independent Challenges, which pose case problems for students to solve. The Independent Challenges allow students to learn by exploring, and develop critical thinking skills. The Visual Workshop that follows the Independent Challenges in Units 2–4 also helps students to develop critical thinking skills. Students are shown a completed worksheet and are asked to recreate it from scratch.

Screen shots — Large-size, full-color representations of what the students' screen should look like after completing the numbered steps.

Related topics — Concise information that either expands on one component of the major lesson skill or describes an independent task that is in some way related to the major lesson skill. These often include both text and screen shots.

Quick Tips and Trouble? — Shortcuts and hints for using Excel 7 more effectively as well as troubleshooting advice to fix common problems that might occur.

CourseTools

CourseTools are Course Technology's way of putting the resources and information needed to teach and learn effectively into your hands. With an integrated array of teaching and learning tools that offer you and your students a broad range of technology-based instructional options, we believe that CourseTools represents the highest quality and most cutting-edge resources available to instructors today. Briefly, the CourseTools available with this text are:

CourseHelp

CourseHelp is a student reinforcement tool offering online annotated tutorials that are accessible directly from the Start menu in Windows 95. These on-screen "slide shows" help students understand the most difficult concepts in a specific application. Students are encouraged to view a CourseHelp before completing that lesson. This text includes the following CourseHelp movies:

- Moving and Copying Text
- Relative versus Absolute Cell Referencing
- Choosing a Chart Type

Adopters of this text are granted the right to post the CourseHelp files on any standalone computer or network.

Student Disk

To use this book students must have a Student Disk. See the inside back cover for more information on the Student Disk. Adopters of this text are granted the right to post the Student Disk on any standalone computer or network.

Course Online Faculty Companion

This new World Wide Web site offers Course Technology customers a password-protected Faculty Lounge where you can find everything you need to prepare for class. These periodically updated items include lesson plans, graphic files for the figures in the text, additional problems, updates and revisions to the text, links to other Web sites, and access to Student Disk files. This new site is an ongoing project and will continue to evolve throughout the semester.

Course Online Student Companion

Our second Web site is a place where students can access challenging, engaging, and relevant exercises. They can find a graphical glossary of terms found in the text, an archive of meaningful templates, software, hot tips, and Web links to other sites as well as sites for specific titles. Student sites can be found at http://www.vmedia.com/cti/. These new sites are also ongoing projects and will continue to evolve throughout the semester.

Instructor's Resource Kit

This is quality assurance tested and includes:

- Solutions to all lessons and end-of-unit material
- Disk containing solutions to all lessons and end-of-unit material
- Unit notes which contain teaching tips from the author
- Extra Independent Challenges
- Transparency Masters of key concepts

Course Test Manager

Designed by Course Technology, this cutting-edge Windows-based testing software helps instructors design and administer tests and pre-tests. This full-featured program also has an online testing component that allows students to take tests at the computer and have their exams automatically graded.

Contents

UNIT 4   Working with Charts   *XL 83*

TABLES

Microsoft® Excel 7
for Windows® 95

Read This Before You Begin
Microsoft Excel 7

To the Student

To complete the step-by-step lessons, Skills Reviews, and Independent Challenges in this book, you must have a Student Disk. See the inside back cover for more information on the Student Disk. See your instructor or technical support person for further information.

 Whenever you see this icon next to a topic, you know that a slideshow movie — called a CourseHelp — is available on that topic. To start a CourseHelp, click the Start button on the taskbar, point to Programs, point to CourseHelp, then click Excel 7 Illustrated Brief. Then, from the CourseHelp opening screen, click the topic that relates to the lesson.

Additional materials designed especially for you are available on the World Wide Web. Go to http://www.vmedia.com/cti/.

Using Your Own Computer

If you are going to work through this book using your own computer, you need a computer system running Microsoft Excel 7 for Windows 95, CourseHelp installed on your computer, and a Student Disk. *You will not be able to complete the step-by-step lessons in this book using your own computer until you have your own Student Disk.* See your instructor for more information on the CourseHelp disk.

To the Instructor

As an adopter of this text, you will receive the CourseHelp disk and the Student Disk. The CourseHelp disk contains a README.DOC file with detailed instructions for installing CourseHelp on a stand-alone machine or on a network. Once installed, students can access CourseHelp movies by clicking the Start button, pointing to Programs, pointing to CourseHelp, and then clicking Excel 7 Illustrated Brief.

The Student Disk contains all the files that students need to complete the step-by-step lessons, Skills Reviews, and Independent Challenges in this book. See the README.DOC file for more information. Your students must have the Student Disk and CourseHelp installed on their computers. See the inside back cover for more information on the Student Disk. You are free to post all these files to a network or stand-alone workstations, or simply to provide copies of the disks to your students.

The instructions in this book assume a standard installation of Microsoft Excel 7 for Windows 95. It is also assumed that the students know which drive and directory contain the Student Disk. It's important that you provide disk location information before the students start working through the units.

UNIT 1

OBJECTIVES

- ▶ Define spreadsheet software
- ▶ Start Excel 7 for Windows 95
- ▶ View the Excel window
- ▶ Work with Excel menus and dialog boxes
- ▶ Work with buttons
- ▶ Get Help
- ▶ Move around the worksheet
- ▶ Name a sheet
- ▶ Close a workbook and exit Excel

Getting Started
WITH MICROSOFT EXCEL 7 FOR WINDOWS 95

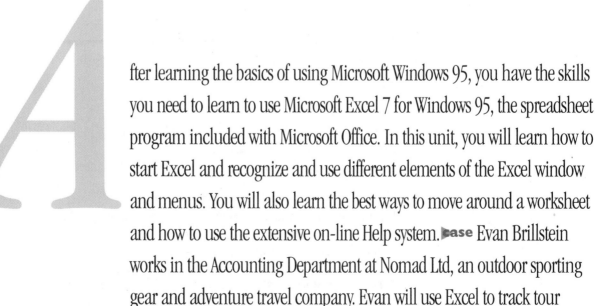

After learning the basics of using Microsoft Windows 95, you have the skills you need to learn to use Microsoft Excel 7 for Windows 95, the spreadsheet program included with Microsoft Office. In this unit, you will learn how to start Excel and recognize and use different elements of the Excel window and menus. You will also learn the best ways to move around a worksheet and how to use the extensive on-line Help system. **Case** Evan Brillstein works in the Accounting Department at Nomad Ltd, an outdoor sporting gear and adventure travel company. Evan will use Excel to track tour sales. ▶

Defining spreadsheet software

Excel is an electronic spreadsheet that runs on Windows computers. An **electronic spreadsheet** uses a computer to perform numeric calculations rapidly and accurately. See Table 1-1 for common ways spreadsheets are used in business. An electronic spreadsheet is also referred to as a **worksheet**, which is the document that you produce when you use Excel. A worksheet created with Excel allows Evan to work quickly and efficiently, and the result produced will be accurate and easily updated. He will be able to produce more professional-looking documents. Figure 1-1 shows a budget worksheet that Evan created using pencil and paper. Figure 1-2 shows the same worksheet that Evan can create using Excel.

Excel is better than the paper system for the following reasons:

■ **Enter data quickly and accurately**
With Excel, Evan can enter information faster and more accurately than he could using the pencil-and-paper method. He only needs to enter data and formulas; Excel calculates the results.

■ **Recalculate easily**
Fixing errors using Excel is easy, and any results based on a changed entry are recalculated automatically.

■ **Perform what-if analysis**
One of the most powerful decision-making features of Excel is the ability to change data and then quickly recalculate changed results. Anytime you use a worksheet to answer the question "what if," you are performing a what-if analysis. For instance, if the advertising budget for May were increased to $3,000, Evan could enter the new figure into the spreadsheet and immediately find out the impact on the overall budget.

■ **Change the appearance of information**
Excel provides powerful features for enhancing a spreadsheet so that information is visually appealing and easy to understand.

■ **Create charts**
Excel makes it easy to create charts based on information in a worksheet. With Excel, charts are automatically updated as data changes. The worksheet in Figure 1-2 includes a pie chart that graphically shows the distribution of expenses for the first quarter.

■ **Share information with other users**
Because everyone at Nomad is now using Microsoft Office, it's easy for Evan to share information with his colleagues. If Evan wants to use the data from someone else's worksheet, he accesses their files through the network or by disk.

■ **Create new worksheets from existing ones quickly**
It's easy for Evan to take an existing Excel worksheet and quickly modify it to create a new one.

FIGURE I-I: Traditional paper worksheet

Nomad Ltd

	Qtr 1	Qtr 2	Qtr 3	Qtr 4	Total
Net Sales	48,000	76,000	64,000	80,000	268,000
Expenses:					
Salary	8,000	8,000	8,000	8,000	32,000
Interest	4,800	5,600	6,400	7,200	24,000
Rent	2,400	2,400	2,400	2,400	9,600
Ads	3,600	8,000	16,000	20,000	47,600
COG	16,000	16,800	20,000	20,400	73,200
Total Exp	34,800	40,800	52,800	58,000	186,400
Net Income	13,200	35,200	11,200	22,000	81,600

FIGURE I-2: Excel worksheet

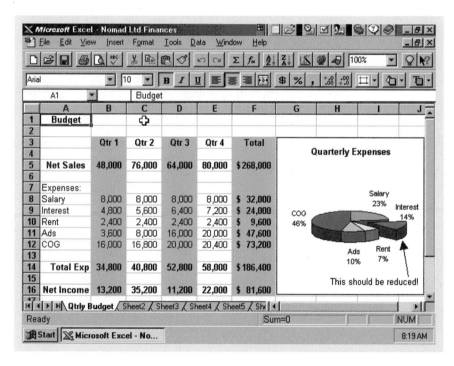

TABLE I-I: Common business spreadsheet uses

USE	SOLUTION
Maintenance of values	Calculation of figures
Visual representation of values	Chart based on worksheet figures

Starting Excel 7 for Windows 95

To start Excel, you use the Windows 95 taskbar. Click Programs, then click the Microsoft Excel program icon. A slightly different procedure might be required for computers on a network and those that use utility programs to enhance Windows 95. If you need assistance, ask your instructor or technical support person for help. **case** Evan starts Excel now.

1 **Locate the Start button on the taskbar**
The Start button is on the left side of the taskbar and is used to start, or **launch**, programs on your computer.

2 **Click the Start button**
Microsoft Excel is located in the Programs group—located at the top of the Start menu, as shown in Figure 1-3.

3 **Point to Programs**
All the programs, or applications, found on your computer can be found in this area of the Start menu.

You can see the Microsoft Excel icon and other Microsoft programs, as shown in Figure 1-4. Your desktop might look different depending on the programs installed on your computer.

4 **Click the Microsoft Excel program icon**
Excel opens and a blank worksheet appears. In the next lesson, you will familiarize yourself with the elements of the Excel worksheet window.

FIGURE 1-3: Start menu

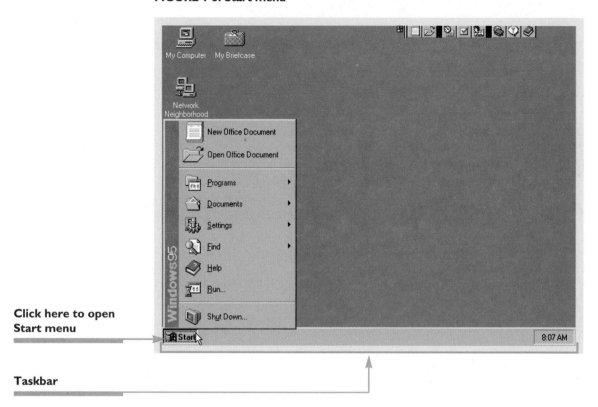

Click here to open Start menu

Taskbar

FIGURE 1-4: Programs available on your computer

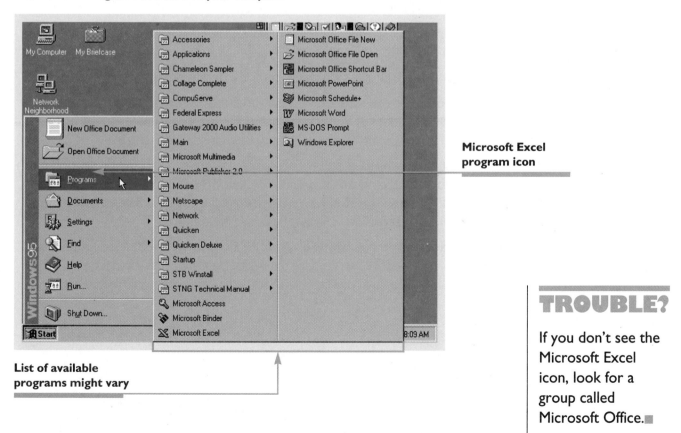

Microsoft Excel program icon

List of available programs might vary

TROUBLE?

If you don't see the Microsoft Excel icon, look for a group called Microsoft Office.■

Viewing the Excel window

When you start Excel, the computer displays the **worksheet window**, the area where you enter data, and the window elements that enable you to create and work with worksheets. Familiarize yourself with the Excel worksheet window and its elements by comparing the descriptions below to Figure 1-5.

■ The **worksheet window** contains a grid of columns and rows. Columns are labeled alphabetically (A, B, C, etc.) and rows are labeled numerically (1, 2, 3, etc.). The worksheet window displays only a tiny fraction of the whole worksheet, which has a total of 256 columns and 16,384 rows. The intersection of a column and a row is a **cell**. Cells can contain text, numbers, formulas, or a combination of all three. Every cell has its own unique location or **cell address**, which is identified by the coordinates of the intersecting column and row. For example, the cell address of the cell in the upper-left corner of a worksheet is A1.

■ The **cell pointer** is a dark rectangle that highlights the cell you are working in, or the **active cell**. In Figure 1-5, the cell pointer is located at A1, so A1 is the active cell. To make another cell active, click any other cell or press the arrow keys on your keyboard to move the cell pointer.

■ The **title bar** displays the program name (Microsoft Excel) and the filename of the open worksheet (in this case, Book1). The title bar also contains a control menu box and resizing buttons.

■ The **menu bar** contains menus from which you choose Excel commands. As with all Windows programs, you can choose a menu command by clicking it with the mouse or by pressing [Alt] plus the underlined letter in the menu name.

■ The **name box** displays the active cell address. In Figure 1-5, "A1" appears in the name box, which means that A1 is the active cell.

■ The **formula bar** allows you to enter or edit data in the worksheet.

■ The **toolbars** contain buttons for the most frequently used Excel commands. To choose a button, simply click it with the left mouse button. The face of any button has a graphic representation of its function; for instance, the printing button has a printer on its face.

■ **Sheet tabs** below the worksheet grid enable you to keep your work in collections called **workbooks**. Each workbook contains 16 worksheets by default and can contain a maximum of 255 sheets. **Sheet tabs** can be given meaningful names. **Sheet tab scrolling buttons** help you move from one sheet to another.

■ The **status bar** is located at the bottom of the Excel window. The left side of the status bar provides a brief description of the active command or task in progress. The right side of the status bar shows the status of important keys, such as the Caps Lock key and the Num Lock key.

FIGURE 1-5: Excel worksheet window elements

Menu bar

Toolbars

Name box

Worksheet window

Sheet tab scrolling
buttons

Cell pointer highlights
active cell, A1

Sheet tabs

Title bar

Formula bar

Status bar

TROUBLE?

If your worksheet
does not fill the
screen as shown in
Figure 1-5, click the
Maximize button
in the worksheet
window.∎

Working with Excel menus and dialog boxes

Like many other Windows programs, Excel provides many commands on its menu bar that you can use to create and format a worksheet. When you choose a menu command that is followed by an ellipsis (...), a **dialog box** opens. A dialog box is a window in which you can specify the options you want for the command. ▶**ase** Evan uses the Format Cells dialog box to enter and format the title for his budget worksheet.

1 Click cell **A1** to make it the active cell if necessary
The cell pointer surrounds A1, and A1 appears in the name box.

2 Type **Budget** then press **[Enter]**
The word "Budget" appears in cell A1, aligned on the left side of the cell. To center this text in the cell, you will use a command from the Format menu.

3 Click cell **A1** then click **Format** on the menu bar
The Format menu opens, displaying a list of commands relating to the appearance of the worksheet. See Figure 1-6. You also could have pressed [Alt][O] to open the Format menu. See the related topic "Using keyboard shortcuts" for more information. Notice that a description of the highlighted menu command displays in the status line. The Cells command has an ellipsis after it, which means that a dialog box will open when Evan chooses this command.

4 Click **Cells**
The Format Cells dialog box opens. See Figure 1-7. Many dialog boxes in Excel have tabs like the workbook tabs. The tabs separate the various formatting options for the selected command into subdialog boxes. The last tab used appears on top. Your screen might display a different tab than the one shown in Figure 1-7.

5 Click the **Alignment tab**
The Alignment tab moves to the front of the dialog box, providing options for changing the alignment of the text in the active cell. Notice the check box next to the Wrap Text option. **Check boxes** toggle an option on or off.

6 In the Horizontal section, click the round circle next to the word "Center"
The round circle is called a **radio button**. Radio buttons display when only one option can be chosen in a section of a dialog box.

7 Click **OK** or press **[Enter]**
If a command button in a dialog box has a dark border around it, you can press [Enter] to choose that button. The dialog box closes and the word "Budget" is centered in cell A1.

FIGURE 1-6: Format menu

Ellipsis (...) indicates a dialog box will open

Format menu

Left-aligned text

Description of highlighted menu command

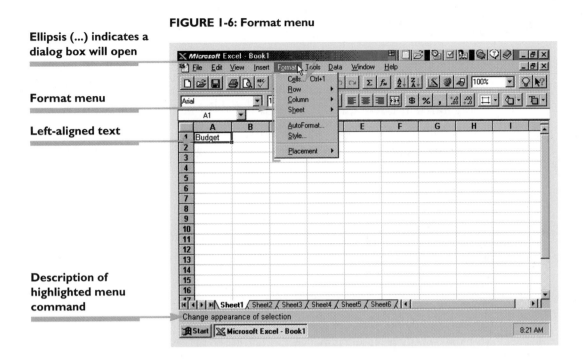

FIGURE 1-7: Format Cells dialog box

Dialog box title bar

Current selection

Dialog box tabs

Dark border means you can press [Enter] to choose command

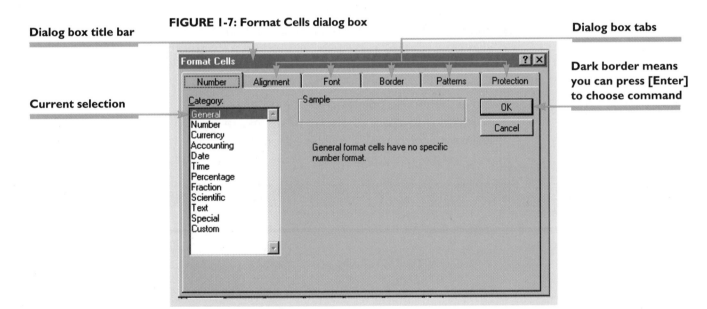

Using keyboard shortcuts

Pointer-movement keys can be used to make choices within a dialog box or menu from the keyboard. To choose a menu from the keyboard, press [Alt] and the underlined letter in the menu you want to select. To choose a menu command from the keyboard, press [↑] or [↓], then press [Enter], or, alternatively, press the underlined letter of the command you want to select. To open a new menu, press [←] or [→]. To move within a dialog box, press the underlined letter of the command you want to execute.

QUICK TIP

To close a menu without choosing a command, click anywhere outside the menu, or press [Esc].■

Working with buttons

Buttons give you easy access to a variety of commonly used Excel commands. Clicking a button to execute a command is faster than using the menu. Buttons are organized in **toolbars**. The Standard and Formatting toolbars are the default toolbars, as shown in Figure 1-8. In addition to these toolbars, Excel provides toolbars that contain buttons for specific purposes such as charting; these will be discussed in future units. You can also customize the toolbars so they contain the buttons for the commands you use most often or reposition them on the screen. See the related topic "Repositioning toolbars" for more information. See Table 1-2 for a description of most frequently used buttons. ►**case** Evan uses the Bold button to format his worksheet title, then explores some of the other buttons.

1 Move the mouse pointer over the Bold button B on the Formatting toolbar, *but do not click the mouse button*
  When you move the pointer over a button, the ToolTip associated with that button appears. The **ToolTip** displays the name of the button, and a description of the button appears in the status bar. See Figure 1-9.

2 Click cell **A1** to make it the active cell, then click B
  The word "Budget" becomes bold. The Bold button is a **toggle button**, which means that if you click the button again, you will undo the last command. Notice that the Center and Bold buttons appear indented, indicating that the cell contents are centered and bold.

3 Move the mouse pointer over the other buttons in the Standard and Formatting toolbars to display the names of these buttons
  Notice how much can be accomplished using buttons.

TABLE 1-2: Frequently used buttons

BUTTON	NAME	DESCRIPTION
	Open	Opens a file
	Save	Saves a file
	Print	Opens the Print dialog box
	Print Preview	Shows the worksheet as it will appear when it is printed
	Spelling	Checks the spelling in the current workbook
	Cut	Cuts the selected range to the Clipboard
	Copy	Copies the selected range to the Clipboard
	Paste	Pastes Clipboard contents into the current workbook at the cell pointer
	Bold	Adds/removes bold formatting

FIGURE 1-8:
Standard and
Formatting toolbars

Standard toolbar

Formatting toolbar

FIGURE 1-9:
Bold ToolTip

Text centered

ToolTip

Center button
indented to indicate it
is activated

Description of
selected button

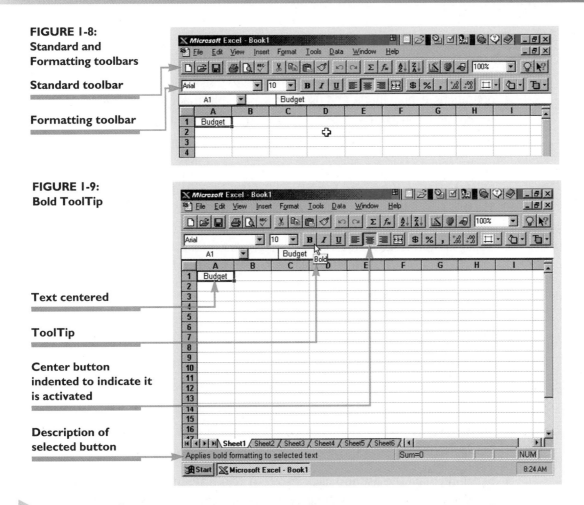

Repositioning toolbars

To allow you to make the best use of your work area, toolbars can be moved and resized. Each toolbar can be positioned along the top of the window, as shown in Figure 1-8, or it can "float" within its own window. To change a toolbar's location, click and hold the pointer in the gray area around the edge of the toolbar, then drag the toolbar away from its current location. To resize a floating toolbar, position the pointer over the edge of the toolbar window until it becomes ←→., then drag the edge until the window is the size you want. In Figure 1-10, the Standard toolbar is floating. Compare Figure 1-10 with Figure 1-9.

FIGURE 1-10:
Standard toolbar
floating

Formatting toolbar

Floating toolbar

Getting Help

Excel features an extensive on-line Help system that gives you immediate access to definitions, explanations, and useful tips. Help information appears in a separate window that you can resize and refer to as you work. ▶case Evan decides to use the on-line Help feature of Excel to learn more about toolbars.

1 Click **Help** on the menu bar, then click **Microsoft Excel Help Topics**
   The Help Topics: Microsoft Excel dialog box opens. This dialog box contains four tabs that provide different ways of getting help. The Index and Find tabs are similar in that you type the topics you are interested in. The Contents tab is similar to a table of contents: it has specific subjects you can look at. Tabs in the Help Topics dialog box are defined in Table 1-3.

2 Click the **Index tab**
   See Figure 1-11. Using the Index tab, you can type a specific topic or feature and view the entries that provide more information.

3 Type **to** in the text box
   Notice as you type each character, the alphabetically arranged topics scroll in the search topics list below the text box. After you type the first "o," "toolbars" appears in the list.

4 Scroll through the list and click **toolbars**, then click **Display**
   A dialog box of additional topics about displaying toolbars opens.

5 Scroll through the list and click **Move a toolbar**, then click **Display**
   The Move a toolbar Help window opens. See Figure 1-12. This window displays information about moving a toolbar. You can click the words with the green-dotted underline (or black-dotted underline, depending on your monitor) to open a pop-up window with more information about that topic.

6 Move the pointer to the dotted-underlined-text **floating toolbar** until the pointer changes to 👆 , then click
   A pop-up window containing a definition of the floating toolbar opens.

7 After reading the information, click anywhere outside the pop-up window or press **[Esc]** to close the pop-up window
   If you want to see additional topics, click Help Topics.

8 Click the **Close button** on the dialog box title bar
   The Help window closes and you return to your worksheet.

FIGURE 1-11: Help Topics: Microsoft Excel dialog box

Type text here

Matching topics display here

FIGURE 1-12: Move a toolbar Help window

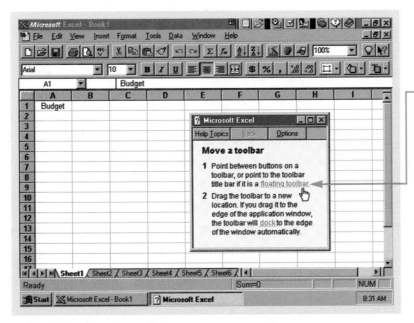

See more information by clicking here

QUICK TIP

If you need help while you are working on a particular topic, click the Help button ![help] on the Standard toolbar. The mouse pointer changes to ![pointer]. Point to a part of the worksheet or a command on a menu, and then click. Excel's Help system displays context-sensitive information about your current location.■

TABLE 1-3: Help tabs

BUTTON	DESCRIPTION
Contents	Displays Help topic categories
Index	Displays an alphabetical listing of topic categories
Find	Displays information based on specific words and phrases
Answer Wizard	Finds information in response to a question format

Moving around the worksheet

With over a billion cells available to you, it's important to know how to move around, or **navigate**, the worksheet. If you want to move up, down, or over one or two cells, you can simply press the pointer-movement keys ([↑] [↓] [←] [→]). To move longer distances within the worksheet window, you might prefer to use the mouse and click the desired cell address. If the desired cell address is not visible within the worksheet window, you can use the scroll bars or the Go To command to move the location into view. Table 1-4 lists helpful techniques for moving around the worksheet. ▶case Evan uses a combination of methods to practice navigating the worksheet.

1   Click cell **I15**
The cell pointer highlights cell I15 in the lower-right corner of your worksheet window.

2   Press **[→]**
The cell pointer moves over one cell to J15, moving the entire worksheet over one column. Notice that cell A1, which contains the word "Budget," is no longer visible in the worksheet window.

3   On the vertical scroll bar, click the **down arrow** once
The worksheet window scrolls down one row, so that row 1 scrolls off the top of the window. You can move a window's contents one row or column at a time by clicking on the vertical or horizontal scroll bar arrows. You can move a screenful at a time by clicking on either side of a scroll box.

4   Click in the area to the right of the horizontal scroll box until column S is displayed
Columns K through S should appear in your worksheet window. If you need to travel a great distance across a worksheet, you can use the Go To command.

5   Click **Edit** on the menu bar, then click **Go To**
The Go To dialog box opens. See Figure 1-13. You could also press [F5] to display the Go To dialog box.

6   Type **Z1000** in the Reference text box, then click **OK**
The cell pointer highlights cell Z1000 in the lower-right corner of the worksheet window. You could use the Go To command or the scroll bars to move the cell pointer back to the beginning of the worksheet, but there is a faster way to move the cell pointer directly to cell A1.

7   Press **[Ctrl][Home]**
The cell pointer highlights cell A1.

FIGURE 1-13: Go To dialog box

Type desired cell
address in text box

TABLE 1-4: Worksheet navigation techniques

TO MOVE	DO THIS
Up one row	Press [↑]
Down one row	Press [↓]
Left one cell	Press [←]
Right one cell	Press[→]
Up one screenful	Press [PgUp]
Down one screenful	Press [PgDn]
Left one screenful	Press [Alt][PgUp]
Right one screenful	Press [Alt][PgDn]
Left one column	Click the left arrow on the horizontal scroll bar
Right one column	Click the right arrow on the horizontal scroll bar
Cell A1	Press [Ctrl][Home]
Column A in current row	Press [Home]
Last active column in current row	Press [End]

Naming a sheet

Each workbook initially contains 16 worksheets. When the workbook is first open, the first worksheet is the active sheet. To move from sheet to sheet, click the desired sheet tab located at the bottom of the worksheet window. Sheet tab scrolling buttons, located to the left of the sheet tabs, allow rapid movement among the sheets. To make it easier to identify the sheets in a workbook, you can name each sheet. The name appears on the sheet tab. For instance, sheets within a single workbook could be named for individual sales people to better track performance goals. ▶case Evan practices moving from sheet to sheet and decides to name two sheets in his workbook.

I **Click the Sheet2 tab**
Sheet2 becomes active. Its tab moves to the front, and the tab for Sheet1 moves to the background. The word "Budget" disappears from view because it is in cell A1 of Sheet1.

2 **Click the Sheet5 tab**
Sheet5 becomes active. Now Evan will rename Sheet1 so it has a name that he can easily remember.

3 **Double-click the Sheet1 tab**
The Rename Sheet dialog box opens with the default sheet name ("Sheet1") selected in the Name text box. You could also click Format in the menu bar, click Sheet, then click Rename to display the Rename Sheet dialog box.

4 **Type Qtrly Budget in the Name text box**
See Figure 1-14. The new name automatically replaced the default name in the Name text box. Worksheet names can have up to 31 characters, including spaces and punctuation.

5 **Click OK**
Notice that the tab of the first sheet says "Qtrly Budget." See Figure 1-15.

6 **Double-click Sheet2 then rename this sheet Additional Info**
You can also rearrange sheets if necessary. See the related topic "Moving sheets" for additional information.

FIGURE 1-14:
Rename Sheet
dialog box

Type new sheet name
here

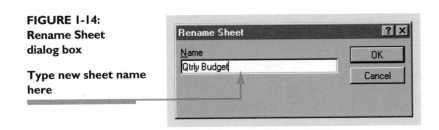

FIGURE 1-15:
Renamed sheet in
workbook

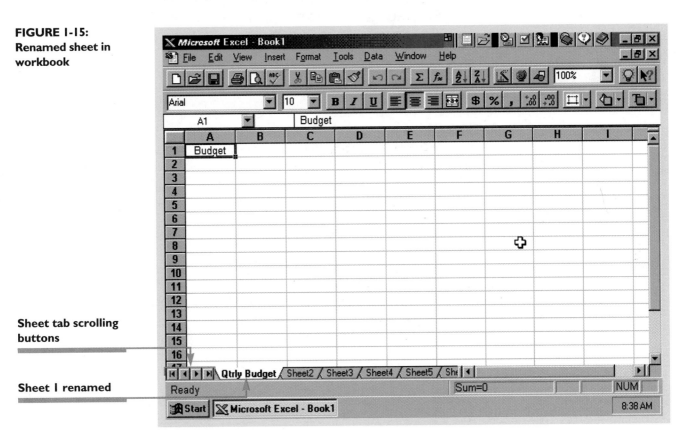

Sheet tab scrolling
buttons

Sheet I renamed

Moving sheets

You can easily rearrange worksheets in a workbook. To move a sheet, position the
mouse pointer on the sheet tab, click and hold the left mouse button, then drag the
sheet tab to its new location. A small arrow and an icon of a document just above
the sheet tabs indicate the new location of the worksheet, as shown in Figure 1-16.

New location indicator

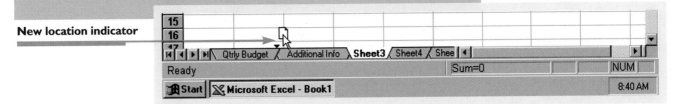

FIGURE 1-16: Moving Sheet3 after Qtrly Budget sheet

Closing a workbook and exiting Excel

When you have finished working on a workbook, you need to save the file and close it. To close a file, click Close on the File menu. When you have completed all your work in Excel, you need to exit the program. To exit Excel, click Exit on the File menu. For a comparison of the Close and Exit commands, refer to Table 1-5. ▶case Evan needs to gather more information before creating his worksheet, so he closes the workbook and then exits Excel.

1 Click **File** on the menu bar
See Figure 1-17.

2 Click **Close**
You could also double-click the workbook control menu box instead of choosing File, Close. In either case, a dialog box opens, asking if you want to save changes in "Book1" before closing. See Figure 1-18. Because he was only practicing, Evan does not want to save the workbook.

3 Click **No**
Excel closes the workbook and displays a blank worksheet window. Notice that the menu bar contains only the File and Help menu choices.

4 Click **File**, then click **Exit**
You could also double-click the program control menu box to exit the program. Excel closes and computer memory is freed up for other computing tasks.

TABLE I-5: Excel's Close and Exit commands

CLOSING A FILE	EXITING EXCEL
Puts away a workbook file	Puts away all workbook files
Leaves Excel running if you choose	Returns you to the desktop where you can choose to run another application

FIGURE 1-17: Closing a workbook using the File menu

Program control
menu box

Workbook control
menu box

Close command

Exit command

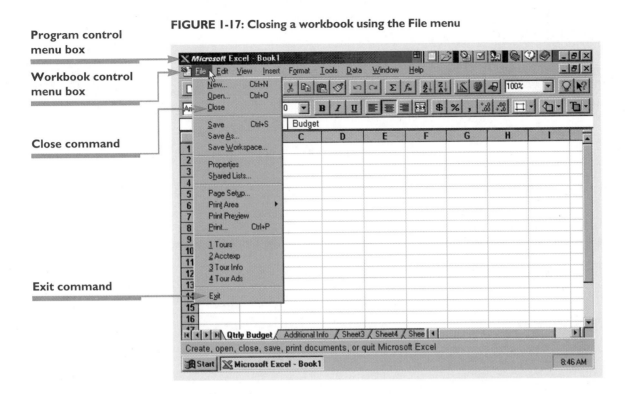

FIGURE 1-18: Microsoft Excel save changes dialog box

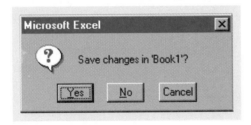

QUICK **TIP**

To exit Excel and
close several files at
once, choose Exit
from the File menu.
Excel will prompt
you to save changes
to each workbook
before exiting.■

TASKREFERENCE

TASK	MOUSE/BUTTON	MENU	KEYBOARD
Close a workbook		Click File, Close	[Alt][F], [C]
Exit Excel		Click File, Exit	[Alt][F], [X]
Make a cell active	Click the cell		[↑], [↓], [←], [→]
Make a choice in a dialog box or menu	Click the desired choice		Press the underlined letter of the command you want to select
Move around the worksheet	Click a cell	Click Edit, Go To	[F5] arrow keys
Move a sheet	Click and drag sheet tab to new location		
Name a sheet	Double-click sheet tab, type name		
Open a dialog box		Click menu command followed by an ellipsis (...)	Press keyboard shortcut for a menu command followed by an ellipsis (...)
Open a menu		Click menu name in the menu bar	[Alt]+underlined letter in menu name
Reposition a toolbar	Click and hold pointer on edge of toolbar, then drag the toolbar to a new location		
Search for Help		Click Help, Search for Help on	[Alt][H], [S]
See a ToolTip	Move the mouse over a button		
Start Excel 95		Click Start button, Programs, Microsoft Office, Microsoft Excel program icon	

CONCEPTSREVIEW

Label each of the elements of the Excel worksheet window shown in Figure 1-19.

1
2
3
4
5
6

FIGURE 1-19

Match each of the terms with the statement that describes its function.

7 Area that contains a grid of columns and rows

8 The intersection of a column and row

9 Graphic symbol that depicts a task or function

10 Collection of worksheets

11 Rectangle that indicates the cell you are currently working in

12 Displays the active cell address

a. Cell pointer

b. Button

c. Worksheet window

d. Name box

e. Cell

f. Workbook

Select the best answer from the list of choices.

13 An electronic spreadsheet can perform all of the following tasks, except:

a. Display information visually

b. Calculate data accurately

c. Plan worksheet objectives

d. Recalculate updated information

14 You can move a screen at a time all of the following ways, except:

a. Press [PgUp]

b. Press [Alt][PgDn]

c. Press [Alt][PgUp]

d. Press [↑]

15 Which key(s) do you press to move quickly to cell A1?

a. [Ctrl][Home]

b. [Alt]

c. [Esc][Home]

d. [Enter]

16 A menu command that is followed by an ellipsis means

a. The command is not currently available.

b. Clicking the command will display a dialog box.

c. Clicking the command will display a submenu.

d. The command has no keyboard shortcut.

17 You can get Excel Help any of the following ways, except by:

a. Clicking Help on the menu bar

b. Pressing [F1]

c. Clicking the Help button on the Standard toolbar

d. Minimizing the application window

18 Which key(s) do you press to move the active cell to the right one column?

a. [Enter]

b. [→]

c. [Esc]

d. [Alt][R]

19 How do you open the Rename Sheet dialog box?

a. Double-click any sheet tab scrolling button.

b. Click the name box list arrow with the right mouse button.

c. Click the Name Sheet Tab button.

d. Double-click the sheet tab.

20 Which key(s) move the cell pointer quickly to the last active column in the current row?

a. [Ctrl][End]

b. [Alt]

c. [End]

d. [Enter]

21 Which of the following statements about buttons is NOT true?

a. You choose a button by clicking it.

b. You move a button by dragging it.

c. A ToolTip, which describes the button, displays when you position the mouse pointer over the button.

d. Buttons appear depressed when selected.

SKILLSREVIEW

1 Start Excel and identify the elements in the worksheet window.

a. Click the Start button.

b. Click the Microsoft Excel program icon.

c. Try to identify as many elements in the Excel worksheet window as you can without referring to the unit material.

2 Explore Excel menus and dialog boxes.

a. Click Edit on the menu bar. Notice that a description of the highlighted Undo command displays in the status bar.

b. Drag through the commands on the Edit menu so that you can review the brief descriptions in the status bar. Press [Esc] if necessary.

c. Click Format on the menu bar.

d. Move through the commands using [↓], and review the descriptions in the status bar.

e. Click Cells on the Format menu to display the Format Cells dialog box. Click each of the tabs and review the options for each tab. Press [Esc] or click cancel.

f. Review other commands on the Excel menu bar in the same fashion.

g. Open the Format Cells dialog box using the keyboard shortcut [Ctrl][1].

h. Close the dialog box by pressing [Esc].

3 Explore buttons.

   a. Position the mouse pointer over each button on the Standard and Formatting toolbars.

   b. Write down each button's function.

   c. Start a list of buttons that duplicate menu commands. Add to this list as you come across more buttons that duplicate menu commands.

   d. Drag the Standard toolbar from its current position so it floats.

   e. Resize the toolbar.

   f. Return the toolbar to its original position.

4 Explore Excel Help.

   a. Click Help on the menu bar.

   b. Click Microsoft Excel Help Topics. The Help Topics: Microsoft Excel dialog box opens.

   c. Identify all of the buttons that appear in the Help Topics: Microsoft Excel dialog box.

   d. Click the down scroll arrow on the search topics list box to view available topics.

   e. Select a topic from the list box, then click Display.

   f. Select a topic to read, then click Display.

   g. Double-click the Help control menu to exit Help.

5 Move around the worksheet.

   a. Press [Ctrl][Home] to move the cell pointer to cell A1.

   b. Press [→] once to move the cell pointer right one column.

   c. Press [↓] twice to move the cell pointer down two rows to cell B3.

   d. Click the right arrow on the horizontal scroll bar to move the screen to the right by one column.

   e. Click the left arrow on the horizontal scroll bar to move the screen back to its original column display.

6 Name a sheet.

   a. Double-click the Sheet3 tab.

   b. Type "January" in the Rename Sheet dialog box, then click OK.

   c. Click the Sheet4 tab.

   d. Click the Sheet2 tab.

   e. Double-click the Sheet1 tab.

   f. Type "February" in the Rename Sheet dialog box, then click OK.

   g. Move the January sheet in front of the February sheet.

7 Close the workbook and exit Excel.

   a. Click File on the menu bar, then click Close.

   b. Click No when asked if you want to save the worksheet.

   c. If necessary, close any other worksheets you might have opened.

   d. Click File on the menu bar, then click Exit.

INDEPENDENT
CHALLENGE I

Excel's on-line Help provides definitions, explanations, procedures, and other helpful information. It also provides examples and demonstrations to show you how Excel features work. Topics include elements such as the active cell, status bar, buttons, and dialog boxes, as well as detailed information about Excel commands and options. To explore Help, click Microsoft Excel Help Topics from the Help menu, click the Contents tab, then read all the information on "Creating, Opening, and Saving Documents" and "Working with Workbooks and Worksheets." Use the Index tab to find information about dialog boxes, the active cell, and the status bar. Return to your workbook when you are finished reading about these Excel features.

INDEPENDENT
CHALLENGE 2

Spreadsheet software has many uses that can affect the way work is done. Some examples of how Excel can be used are discussed in the beginning of this unit. Use your own personal or business experiences to come up with five examples of how Excel could be used in a business setting.

To complete this independent challenge:

1 Think of five business tasks that you could complete more efficiently by using an Excel worksheet.

2 Sketch a sample of each worksheet. See Figure 1-20, which is an example of a payroll worksheet.

3 Submit your sketches.

Employee Names	Hours Worked	Hourly Wage	Gross Pay	
Janet Bryce			→	Gross pay=
Anthony Krups			→	Hours worked
Grant Miller			→	times
Barbara Salazar			→	Hourly wage
Total	↓	↓	↓	

FIGURE I-20

UNIT 2

Creating A WORKSHEET

Now that you are familiar with Excel menus, dialog boxes, tools, and the on-line Help system and you know how to navigate within an Excel workbook, you are ready to plan and build your own worksheets. When you build a worksheet, you enter text, values, and formulas into worksheet cells. Once you create a worksheet, you can save it in a workbook file and then print it. Helping managers plan for the future is one of the many ways Excel is useful for businesses. **case** Evan Brillstein has received a request from the Marketing Department for a forecast of this year's anticipated summer tour business. Marketing hopes that the tour business will increase 20% over last year's figures. ▶

Planning and designing a worksheet

Before you start entering data into a worksheet, you need to know the purpose and approximate layout of the worksheet. Evan wants to forecast Nomad's 1996 summer tour sales. The sales goal, already identified by the Marketing Department, is to increase the 1995 summer sales by 20%. **case** Using Figure 2-1 and the planning guidelines below, follow Evan as he plans his worksheet.

■ **Determine the purpose of the worksheet and give it a meaningful title.**
Evan needs to forecast summer tour sales for 1996. Evan titles the worksheet "1996 Summer Tour Sales Forecast."

■ **Determine your worksheet's desired results, sometimes called output.**
Evan needs to determine what the 1996 sales totals will be if sales increase by 20% over the 1995 sales totals.

■ **Collect all the information, sometimes called input, that will produce the results you want to see.**
Evan gathers together the sales data for the 1995 summer tour season. The season ran from June through August. The types of tours sold in these months included Bike, Raft, Horse, and Bus.

■ **Determine the calculations, or formulas, necessary to achieve the desired results.**
First, Evan needs to total the number of tours sold for each month of the 1995 summer season. Then he needs to add these totals together to determine the grand total of summer tour sales. Finally, the 1995 monthly totals and grand total must be multiplied by 1.2 to calculate a 20% increase for the 1996 summer tour season.

■ **Sketch on paper how you want the worksheet to look; that is, identify where the labels and values will go. Labels are text entries that describe and help you understand the data in a worksheet. Values are the numbers used in calculations.**
Evan decides to put tour types in rows and the months in columns. He enters the tour sales data in his sketch and indicates where the monthly sales totals and the grand total should go. Below the totals, he writes out the formula for determining a 20% increase in sales for 1996. Evan's sketch of his worksheet is shown in Figure 2-1.

FIGURE 2-1: Worksheet sketch showing labels, values, and calculations

1996 Summer Tours Sales Forecast

	June	July	August	Totals
Bike	14	10	6	3 month total
Raft	7	8	12	
Horse	12	7	6	
Bus	1	2	9	↓
Totals	June Total	July Total	August Total	Grand Total for 1995
1996 Sales	Total x 1.2			→

Entering labels

Labels are used to identify the data in the rows and columns of a worksheet. They are also used to make your worksheet readable and understandable. For these reasons, you should enter all labels in your worksheet first. Labels can contain text and numerical information not used in calculations, such as dates, times, or address numbers. Labels are left-aligned by default. ▶︎**ase** Using his sketch as a guide, Evan begins building his worksheet by entering the labels.

1 **Start Excel and make sure you have an empty workbook in the Excel worksheet window**
   If you need help starting Excel, refer to the lesson "Starting Excel 7 for Windows 95" in Unit 1.

2 **Click cell B4 to make it the active cell**
   Notice that the cell address B4 appears in the name box. Now Evan enters the worksheet title.

3 **Type 1996 Summer Tours Sales Forecast, as shown in Figure 2-2, then click the Enter button ☑ on the formula bar**
   You must click ☑ or use one of the other methods listed in Table 2-1 to confirm your entry. Notice that the title does not fit in cell B4 and spreads across several columns. If a label does not fit in a cell, Excel displays the remaining characters in the next cell as long as it is empty. Otherwise, the label is **truncated**, or cut off. The contents of B4, the active cell, display in the formula bar. When a cell contains both text and numbers, Excel recognizes the entry as a label. If you want to enter a number as a label, you would type an apostrophe (') before the first number.

4 **Click cell A6, type Bike, then press [Enter] to complete the entry and move the cell pointer to cell A7; type Raft in cell A7, then press [Enter]; type Horse in cell A8, then press [Enter]; then type Bus in cell A9, then press [Enter]**
   Now Evan enters the labels for the rows containing the totals and the 1996 sales forecast.

5 **Click cell A11, type Total, then press [Enter]; click cell A13, type 1996 Sales, then press [Enter]**
   Next he enters the labels for the summer months.

6 **Click cell B5, type June, then click ☑; click cell C5, type July, then click ☑; click cell D5, type August, then click ☑**

7 **Click cell E5, type Total, then click ☑**
   All the labels for Evan's worksheet are now entered. See Figure 2-3.

FIGURE 2-2: Worksheet with title entered

Formula bar

Name box

Enter button

Title spreads across columns

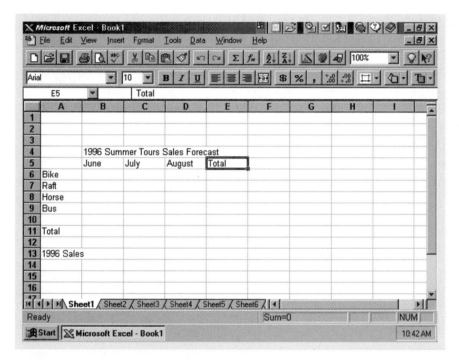

FIGURE 2-3: Worksheet with labels entered

TABLE 2-1: Confirming cell entries

ACTION	CONFIRMS ENTRY THEN
Click ☑	Cell pointer stays in current cell
Press [Enter]	Cell pointer moves one row down
Press [Shift][Enter]	Cell pointer moves one row up
Press [Tab]	Cell pointer moves one column to the right
Press [Shift][Tab]	Cell pointer moves one column to the left
Click in another cell or press [↑], [↓], [←], or [→]	Cell pointer moves to the cell that is clicked, or one cell in the direction indicated

TROUBLE?

If you notice a mistake in a cell entry after it has been confirmed, select the cell you want to edit and press [F2]. Use [Backspace] and/or [Delete] to make any corrections, then click ☑ or press [Enter] to confirm the corrected entry.■

Entering values

Values, which include numbers, formulas, and functions, are used in calculations. Excel recognizes an entry as a value when it is a number or begins with one of these symbols: +, -, =, @, #, or $. All values are right-aligned by default. ▶case Evan enters the sales data from the 1995 summer season into his worksheet.

1 Click cell **B6**, type **14**, then press **[Enter]**; type **7** in cell B7, then press **[Enter]**; type **12** in cell B8, then press **[Enter]**; type **1** in cell B9, then press **[Enter]**

   All the tour sales for the month of June are now entered. Now Evan enters the sales for the month of July.

2 Click cell **C6**, type **10**, then press **[Enter]**; type **8** in cell C7, then press **[Enter]**; type **7** in cell C8, then press **[Enter]**; type **2** in cell C9, then press **[Enter]**

   Next he enters the tour sales for August.

3 Click cell **D6**, type **6**, then press **[Enter]**; type **12** in cell D7, then press **[Enter]**; type **6** in cell D8, then press **[Enter]**; type **9** in cell D9, then press **[Enter]**

   Evan has entered all the labels and data he needs for his worksheet. Compare your worksheet to Figure 2-4.

FIGURE 2-4: Worksheet with labels and values entered

Labels

Values

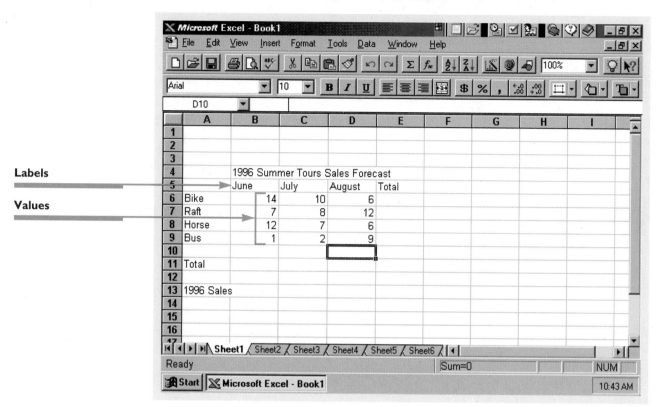

Editing cell entries

You can change the contents of any cells at any time. To edit the contents of a cell, you first select the cell you want to edit, then click the formula bar, double-click the selected cell, or press [F2]. This puts Excel into Edit mode. To make sure you are in Edit mode, check the mode indicator on the far left of the status bar. Refer to Table 2-2 for more information on the mode indicator. ►case After checking his worksheet, Evan notices that he entered the wrong value for the June bus tours and forgot to include the canoe tours. He fixes the bus tours figure, and he decides to add the canoe sales data to the raft sales figures.

1 Click cell **B9**
This cell contains June bus tours, which Evan needs to change to 2.

2 Click anywhere in the formula bar
Excel goes into Edit mode, and the mode indicator displays "Edit." The **AutoCalculate** field on the status bar displays the formula in the cell; in this case, SUM=1 is displayed. A blinking vertical line, called the **insertion point**, appears in the formula bar, and if you move the mouse pointer to the formula bar, the pointer changes to I. See Figure 2-5.

3 Press **[Backspace]**, type **2**, then press **[Enter]** or click the **Enter button** ☑ on the formula bar
Evan now needs to add "/Canoe" to the Raft label.

4 Click cell **A7** then press **[F2]**
Excel is in Edit mode again, but the insertion point is in the cell.

5 Type **/Canoe** then press **[Enter]**
The label changes to Raft/Canoe, which is a little too long to fit in the cell. Don't worry about this. You will learn how to change the width of a column later.

6 Double-click cell **B7**
Double-clicking a cell also puts Excel into Edit mode with the insertion point in the cell.

7 Press **[Delete]** then type **9**
See Figure 2-6.

8 Click ☑ to confirm the entry
You can also cancel the entry if you notice a mistake. See the related topic "Using the Cancel button" for more information.

TABLE 2-2:
Understanding the mode indicator

MODE	DESCRIPTION
Edit	You are editing a cell entry
Enter	You are entering data
Error	You have made an entry Excel cannot understand; click the Help button ☒ on the Standard toolbar or click OK
Point	You have specified a range without a formula
Ready	Excel is ready for you to enter data or choose a command
Wait	Excel is completing a task

FIGURE 2-5: Worksheet in Edit mode

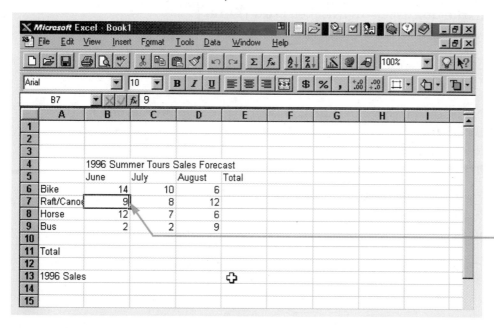

Insertion point in formula bar

Mouse pointer

AutoCalculate field displays sum in active cell

Edit mode indicator

FIGURE 2-6: Worksheet with edits completed

Insertion point in cell

Using the Cancel button

When you enter data into a cell, the Cancel button ☒ appears immediately to the left of the Enter button ☑ on the formula bar. If you make a mistake entering data or editing a cell entry, you can click ☒ instead of confirming the entry. This removes the data entered, and the cell reverts to its original contents.

QUICK TIP

If you make a mistake, click the Undo button on the Standard toolbar ☜ or choose Undo from the Edit menu before doing anything else.■

Working with ranges

Any group of cells (two or more) is called a **range**. To select a range, click the first cell and drag to the last cell you want included in the range. The range address is defined by noting the first and last cells in the range. Figure 2-7 shows a selected range whose range address is B6:C9. You can give a meaningful name to a range and then use the range name in formulas. Range names are usually easier to remember than cell addresses and they also help you move around the workbook quickly. See the related topic "Using range names to move around a workbook" for more information. ▶**ase** To make his forecasting worksheet easier to under-stand, Evan decides to use range names in the worksheet.

1 Click cell **B6** then drag to cell **B9** to select the range B6:B9

2 Click the **name box** to name the cell range B6:B9

3 Type **June** then press **[Enter]**
Now whenever cells B6:B9 are selected, the range name "June" will appear in the name box.

4 Click cell **C6** then drag to cell **C9** to select the range C6:C9; click the **name box**, type **July**, then press **[Enter]**

5 Click cell **D6** then drag to cell **D9** to select the range D6:D9; click the **name box**, type **August**, then press **[Enter]**
Next, Evan names the four ranges containing the data for each type of tour.

6 Select the range **B6:D6**, click the **name box**, type **Bike**, then press **[Enter]**

7 Name the range B7:D7 **RaftCanoe**, range B8:D8 **Horse**, and range B9:D9 **Bus**
Note that there is no slash separating the words "Raft" and "Canoe" in the range name for the range B7:D7.

8 Click the **name box list arrow** to see the list of range names in this worksheet
Notice that the named ranges are in alphabetical order. See Figure 2-8.

9 Click anywhere outside the range name list to close it

FIGURE 2-7: Worksheet showing selected range of cells

Name box

Selected range

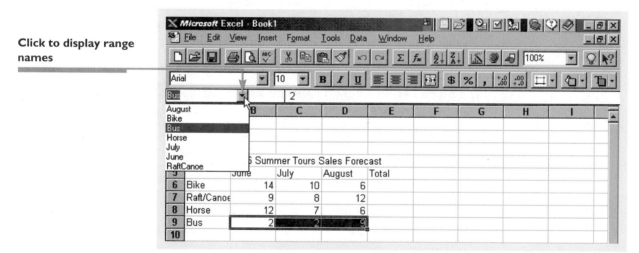

FIGURE 2-8: List of range names

Click to display range names

Using range names to move around a workbook

You can use range names to move around a workbook quickly. Click the name box list arrow, then click the name of the range you want to go to, as shown in Figure 2-9. The cell pointer moves immediately to that range.

August range selected

Cell pointer moves to selected range

FIGURE 2-9:
Moving the cell pointer using range names

Entering formulas

Formulas are used to perform numeric calculations such as adding, multiplying, and averaging. Formulas in an Excel worksheet start with the formula prefix—the equal sign (=). All formulas use **arithmetic operators** to perform calculations. See Table 2-3 for a list of Excel operators. Formulas often contain cell addresses and range names. Using a cell address or range name in a formula is called **cell referencing**. Using cell references keeps your worksheet up-to-date and accurate. If you change a value in a cell, any formula containing that cell reference will be automatically recalculated using the new value. ▶ case Evan uses formulas to add the monthly tour totals for June, July, and August.

1 Click cell **B11**
This is the cell where Evan wants to put the calculation that will total the June sales.

2 Type = (the equal sign)
The equal sign at the beginning of an entry tells Excel that a formula is about to be entered rather than a label or a value. The total June sales is equal to the sum of the values in cells B6, B7, B8, and B9.

3 Type **b6+b7+b8+b9** then click the **Enter button** 🗹 on the formula bar
The result of 37 appears in cell B11, and the formula appears in the formula bar. See Figure 2-10. Next, Evan adds the number of tours in July.

4 Click cell **C11**, type **=c6+c7+c8+c9**, then click 🗹
The result of 27 appears in C11. Finally, Evan enters the formula to calculate the August tour sales.

5 Click cell **D11**, type **=d6+d7+d8+d9**, then click 🗹
The total tour sales for August appear in cell D11. Compare your results with Figure 2-11.

TABLE 2-3: Excel arithmetic operators

OPERATOR	PURPOSE	EXAMPLE
+	Performs addition	=A5+A7
−	Performs subtraction	=A5-10
*	Performs multiplication	=A5*A7
/	Performs division	=A5/A7

FIGURE 2-10: Worksheet showing formula and result

FIGURE 2-11: Worksheet with formulas for monthly totals entered

Formula in formula bar

Calculated result
in cell

TROUBLE?

If the formula
instead of the result
appears in the cell
after you click ▣,
make sure you began
the formula with =
(the equal sign).■

Entering formulas, continued

Formulas can contain more than one arithmetic operator. In these situations, Excel decides which operation to perform first. See the related topic "Order of precedence in Excel formulas" for more information. ▶**ase** Now that Evan has calculated the monthly total tour sales for 1995, he can use these figures to calculate the forecast for 1996. He will use the multiplication symbol, * (the asterisk), to write the formula calculating a 20% increase of 1995 sales. This time he will click the cell address to be included in the formula rather than typing it.

6 Click cell **B13**, type =, click cell **B11**, type ***1.2**, then click ☑ on the formula bar
   To calculate the 20% increase, you multiply the total by 1.2. This formula calculates the result of multiplying the total monthly tour sales for June, cell B11, by 1.2. The result of 44.4 appears in cell B13.

   Now Evan calculates the 20% increase for July and August.

7 Click cell **C13**, type =, click cell **C11**, type ***1.2**, then click ☑

8 Click cell **D13**, type =, click cell **D11**, type ***1.2**, then click ☑
   Compare your results with Figure 2-12.

FIGURE 2-12: Calculated results for 20% increase

Order of precedence in Excel formulas

Each of the formulas for Evan's calculations involves only one arithmetic operator, but a formula can include several operations. When you work with formulas that have more than one operator, the **order of precedence** is very important. If a formula contains two or more operators, such as 4 + .55/4000 * 25, the computer performs the calculations in a particular sequence based on these rules:

Calculated 1st   Calculation of exponents

Calculated 2nd   Multiplication and division, left to right

Calculated 3rd   Addition and subtraction, left to right

In the example 4 + .55/4000 * 25, Excel performs the arithmetic operations in the following order. First, 4000 is divided into .55. Next Excel multiplies the result of .55/4000 by 25, then adds 4 to the result. You can change the order of calculations by using parentheses. Operations inside parentheses are calculated before any other operations.

Using Excel functions

Functions are predefined worksheet formulas that enable you to do complex calculations easily. Functions always begin with the formula prefix = (the equal sign). You can enter functions manually, or you can use the Function Wizard. See the related topic "Using the Function Wizard" for more information. ▶ase Evan uses the SUM function to calculate the grand totals in his worksheet. See Table 2-4 for a listing of frequently used functions.

1 Click cell **E6**
This is the cell where Evan wants to display the total of all bike tours for June, July, and August.

2 Position the pointer over the **AutoSum button** 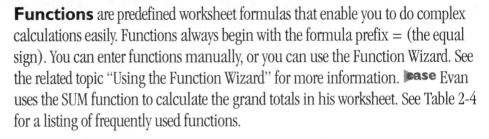 on the Standard toolbar
See Figure 2-13. AutoSum sets up the SUM function to add the values in the cells above the cell pointer. If there are no values in the cells above the cell pointer, AutoSum adds the values in the cells to the left of the cell pointer—in this case, the values in cells B6, C6, and D6.

3 Click Σ
The formula =SUM(B6:D6) appears in the formula bar. The information inside the parentheses is the argument. An **argument** can be a value, a range of cells, text, or another function. After verifying that Excel has selected the correct range, Evan confirms the entry.

4 Click the **Enter button** ▦ on the formula bar
The result appears in cell E6. Next Evan calculates the total of raft and canoe tours.

5 Click cell **E7**, click Σ, then click ▦
Now he calculates the three-month total of the horse tours.

6 Click cell **E8** then click Σ
AutoSum sets up a function to sum the two values in the cells above the active cell. Evan needs to change the argument.

7 Click cell **B8** then drag to select the range B8:D8
As you drag, the argument in the SUM function changes to reflect the range being chosen.

8 Click ▦ to confirm the entry

9 Enter the SUM function in cells E9, E11, and E13
Make sure you add the values to the left of the active cell, not the values above it. See Figure 2-14.

TABLE 2-4: Frequently used functions

FUNCTION	DESCRIPTION
SUM(*argument*)	Calculates the sum of the arguments
AVERAGE(*argument*)	Calculates the average of the arguments
MAX(*argument*)	Displays the largest value among the arguments
MIN(*argument*)	Displays the smallest value among the arguments
COUNT(*argument*)	Calculates the number of values in the arguments

FIGURE 2-13:
AutoSum button

AutoSum ToolTip

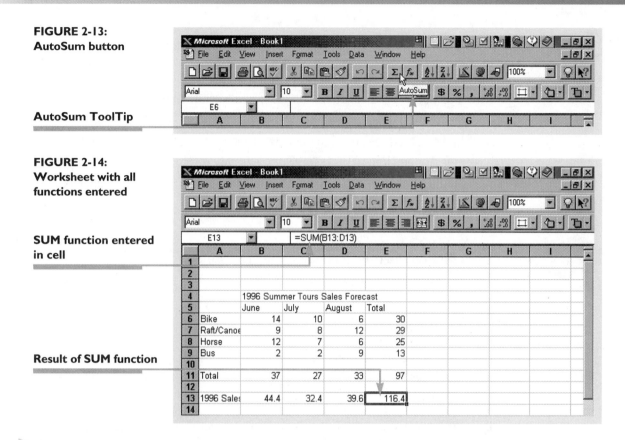

FIGURE 2-14:
Worksheet with all
functions entered

SUM function entered
in cell

Result of SUM function

Using the Function Wizard

The Function Wizard button [fx] is located to the right of the AutoSum button on the Standard toolbar. To use the Function Wizard, click [fx]. In the Function Wizard - Step 1 of 2 dialog box, shown in Figure 2-15, click the category containing the function you want, then click the desired function. The function appears in the formula bar. Click Next to display the Function Wizard - Step 2 of 2 dialog box, fill in values or cell addresses for the arguments, then click Finish.

Function Wizard
button

Functions and
arguments appear
in formula bar

Description of
selected function

Click to fill in
arguments

FIGURE 2-15: First Function Wizard dialog box

QUICK **TIP**

If you are not sure what a specific function does, use the Function Wizard to see a description of its function.■

Saving a workbook

To store the workbook permanently, you must save it to a file on a disk. You should save your work every 10 to 15 minutes, especially before making significant changes in a workbook and before printing. You will create the My Excel Files folder on your Student Disk, then save this file there. For more information about your Student Disk, refer to the "Read This Before You Begin Microsoft Excel 7" page. Important files should be copied onto a different disk for safekeeping. See the related topic "Filenames and extensions" for more information on file-naming conventions. ▶**case** Evan wants to save his work.

1 Click **File** on the main menu bar, then choose **Save As**
The Save As dialog box opens. See Figure 2-16. The text in the File name text box is already selected.

2 Insert your Student Disk in the appropriate drive

3 Click the **Save in list arrow**, then click **3 ½ Floppy (A:)**
These lessons assume that your Student Disk is in drive A. If you are using a different drive or storing your practice files on a network, click the appropriate drive.

Create a new folder where you will save your Excel work files.

4 Click the **Create New Folder button** ⬜, type **My Excel Files** in the Name box, then click **OK**
Once the new folder is created, you must make it active (so it displays in the Save in text box); then you can name your file.

5 Double-click the **My Excel Files folder**, double-click **Book1** in the File name box, then type **Tours**
Excel automatically adds the .xls extension to the filename, although it is not displayed in the title bar.

6 Click **Save**
The Save As dialog box closes, and the filename appears in the title bar at the top of the workbook.

The workbook is saved to the My Excel Files folder on your Student Disk as a file named Tours.xls (although the .xls does not appear in the title bar). Next, Evan enters his name at the top of the worksheet, so that if others who use this worksheet have questions about it, they can ask him.

7 Click cell **A2**, type **Evan Brillstein**, then press **[Enter]**

8 Click **File** on the menu bar, then click **Save**
This saves the changes made to a file that has already been named. Save a file frequently while working on it to protect all data. Table 2-5 shows the difference between the Save and the Save As commands.

FIGURE 2-16: Save As dialog box

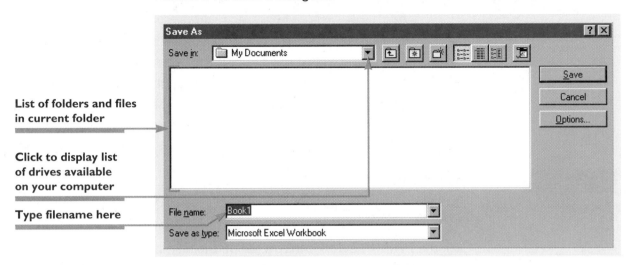

List of folders and files in current folder

Click to display list of drives available on your computer

Type filename here

Filenames and extensions

When you save a file, Excel automatically adds the extension .xls to the filename. Unlike previous versions of Excel, the extension does not display in the title bar and does not appear to the right of the filename in the Windows Explorer. Windows 95 allows you to have filenames up to 255 characters in length. Filenames can use lower or uppercase letters, numbers, symbols, and spaces.

TABLE 2-5: Difference between Save and Save As commands

COMMAND	DESCRIPTION	PURPOSE
Save As	Saves file, requires input name	To save a file the first time, to change the filename, or to save the file for use in a different program; useful for backup copies of files
Save	Saves named file	To save any changes to the original file; fast and easy—do this often to protect your work

Previewing and printing a worksheet

When a worksheet is completed, you print it to have a paper copy to reference, file, or send to others. You can also print a worksheet that is not complete to review it or work on when you are not at a computer. Before you print a worksheet, you should preview it to make sure that it will fit on a page. When you preview a worksheet, you see a copy of the worksheet exactly as it will appear on paper. Table 2-6 provides printing tips. ▶ase Evan previews and then prints a copy of the Tours worksheet.

1 Make sure the printer is on and contains paper
   If a file is sent to print and the printer is off, an error message appears. Evan previews the worksheet to check its overall appearance.

2 Click the **Print Preview button** 🔍 on the Standard toolbar
   You could also click File on the menu bar, then click Print Preview. A miniature version of the worksheet appears on the screen, as shown in Figure 2-17. If there were more than one page, you could click Next and Previous to move between pages. You can also enlarge the image by clicking the Zoom button. See the related topic "Using Zoom in Print Preview" for more information. After verifying that the preview image is correct, Evan prints the worksheet.

3 Click **Print**
   The Print dialog box opens, as shown in Figure 2-18.

4 Make sure that the **Selected Sheet(s) radio button** is selected and that
   1 appears in the Number of Copies text box
   Now Evan is ready to print the worksheet.

5 Click **OK**
   The Printing dialog box appears while the file is sent to the printer. Note that the dialog box contains a Cancel button that you can use to cancel the print job.

6 Click **File** on the menu bar, then click **Close** to close the workbook

7 Click **File** on the menu bar, then click **Exit**
   Excel closes and you are returned to the desktop window.

TABLE 2-6: Worksheet printing tips

BEFORE YOU PRINT	RECOMMENDATION
Check the printer	Make sure that the printer is on and online, that it has paper, and that there are no error messages or warning signals
Preview the worksheet	Check the formatted image for page breaks, page setup (vertical or horizontal), and overall appearance of the worksheet
Check the printer selection	Use the Printer setup command in the Print dialog box to verify that the correct printer is selected

FIGURE 2-17:
Print Preview screen

Move to another page

Enlarge the screen
image

Print the worksheet

Change print options

Return to worksheet

Mouse pointer

FIGURE 2-18:
Print dialog box

Choose to print the
current worksheet

Set the number of
copies here

Using Zoom in Print Preview

When you are in the Print Preview window, you can make the image of the page
larger by clicking the Zoom button. You can also position the mouse pointer over
a specific part of the worksheet page, then click it to view that section of the page.
While the image is zoomed in, use the scroll bars to view different sections of the
page. See Figure 2-19.

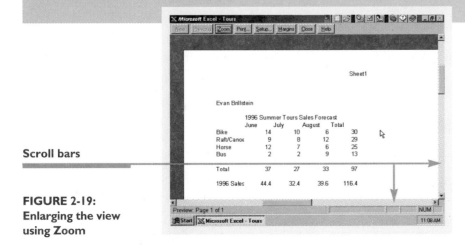

Scroll bars

FIGURE 2-19:
Enlarging the view
using Zoom

QUICK **TIP**

You should save
your worksheet
prior to printing;
then, if anything
happens to the file
as it is being sent to
the printer, you will
have a clean copy
saved to your disk.

TASKREFERENCE

TASK	MOUSE/BUTTON	MENU	KEYBOARD
Accept an entry	✓		[Enter]
Add a range	Σ		Type =SUM function
Cancel an entry	✗		[Esc]
Edit cell entry	Click formula bar		[F2]
Go to a named range	Click Name box arrow	Click Edit, Go To	[F5]
Make a value entry a label			Type ' before entering value
Name a range	Click Name box	Click Insert, Name, Define	[Alt][I],[N],[D]
Preview a worksheet	🔍	Click File, Print Preview	[Alt][F][V]
Print a worksheet	🖨	Click File, Print	[Ctrl][P]
Save a workbook	💾	Click File, Save	[Ctrl][S]
Undo an entry	↺	Click Edit, Undo	[Ctrl][Z]
Use a function	fx	Click Insert, Function	[Alt][I],[F]

CONCEPTSREVIEW

Label each of the elements of the Excel worksheet window shown in Figure 2-20.

1
2
3
4
5
6
7

FIGURE 2-20

Match each of the terms with the statement that describes its function.

8 A predefined formula that provides a shortcut for commonly used calculations

9 A cell entry that performs a calculation in an Excel worksheet

10 A specified group of cells, which can include the entire worksheet

11 The location of a particular cell in a worksheet, identified by a column letter and row number

12 The character that identifies a value as a label

a. Range

b. Function

c. Cell address

d. Apostrophe

e. Formula

Select the best answer from the list of choices.

13 All of the following confirm an entry in a cell except:

a. Clicking the Cancel button

b. Clicking the Enter button

c. Pressing [Enter]

d. Pressing [↓]

14 The first character in any Excel formula is

a. *

b. /

c. =

d. @

SKILLSREVIEW

1 Enter labels and save a workbook.

  a. Start Excel and make sure you have an empty workbook in the Excel worksheet window.

  b. Name Sheet1 tab "Funds."

  c. Save the workbook as Funds to the My Excel Files folder on your Student Disk.

  d. Type "Total" in cell A6, then press [Enter].

  e. Click cell B1 then type "Shares."

  f. Click ☑ on the formula bar to enter Shares in cell B1.

  g. Press [→] to move to C1, then type "Price."

  h. Press [Tab] to move to cell D1.

  i. Type "Sold" and then press [Esc]. Note that the entry disappears from the cell. Leave cell D1 blank.

  j. Save your work.

2 Enter values and name ranges.

  a. Enter the four mutual funds labels and values from Table 2-7 into the range A1:C5 in the Funds worksheet.

TABLE 2-7		
	SHARES	PRICE
Arch	210	10.01
RST	50	18.45
United	100	34.50
Vista	65	11.15

  b. Name range B2:B5 "Shares."

  c. Name range C2:C5 "Price."

  d. Save, then preview and print the worksheet.

3 Enter formulas, then preview and print the worksheet.

  a. Click cell B6.

  b. Enter the formula B2+B3+B4+B5.

  c. Click the name box, then click Price.

  d. Save your work, then preview and print the data in the Funds worksheet.

4 Use Excel functions.

  a. Click cell C7.

  b. Enter the function AVERAGE(C2:C5).

  c. Type the label "Average Price" in cell A7.

  d. Save your work.

  e. Preview and print this worksheet.

  f. Close the workbook.

5 Build a simple check register to balance a checkbook. Set up the worksheet using the data from Table 2-8 in a new workbook.

TABLE 2-8			
CHECK NO.	DATE	DESC.	AMOUNT
1601	June 17	Cleaning	12.65
1602	June 29	Tickets	38.02
1603	July 18	Cable	14.50
1604	July 25	Food	47.98

  a. Click the New Workbook button ▢ to open a new workbook.

  b. Name Sheet1 tab "Checkbook."

  c. Enter the label "Check Register" in cell A1.

  d. Enter the column labels in the range A3:D3.

  e. Enter all four check numbers, with the corresponding dates, descriptions, and amounts in the range A4:D7. Don't worry if the format of the date entries changes.

  f. Generate a total of the check amounts you have entered. Enter the function SUM(D4:D7) in cell D8. Enter the label "Total" in cell A8.

  g. Save the workbook as Checks to the My Excel Files folder on your Student Disk. Then preview and print the worksheet.

6 Edit cell entries and preview the worksheet.

a. The description for check 1601 should be "Laundry."

b. Click cell D5, click in the formula bar, then change the amount for check 1602 to "43.62."

c. Click cell D6, press [F2], then change the amount for check 1603 to "23.22."

d. Save your work, preview and print the worksheet, then close the workbook.

7 Develop a worksheet that calculates the weekly payroll for Suncoast Security Systems. Open a new workbook and set up the worksheet using the data from Table 2-9.

TABLE 2-9			
EMPLOYEE	HOURS WORKED	HOURLY WAGE	GROSS PAY
D. Hillman	32	9	
S. Lipski	25	12	
L. Skillings	40	7	

a. Click the New Workbook button ▣ to open a new workbook.

b. Enter the column labels, beginning in cell A2. Use two rows for the labels.

c. Enter the employee names, hours worked, and wage information using Table 2-9.

d. Use the Function Wizard to calculate the total of cells B4:B6 in cell B7 (the total hours worked).

e. Name Sheet1 tab "Suncoast."

f. Save your workbook as Suncoast Security to the My Excel Files folder on your Student Disk.

g. Preview the worksheet, use the Zoom feature to enlarge the image, and then print the worksheet.

INDEPENDENT
CHALLENGE 1

You are the box-office manager for Lightwell Players, a regional theater company. Your responsibilities include tracking seasonal ticket sales for the company's main stage productions and anticipating ticket sales for the next season. Lightwell Players sells four types of tickets: reserved seating, general admission, senior citizen tickets, and student tickets.

The 1993–94 season included productions of *Hamlet*, *The Cherry Orchard*, *Fires in the Mirror*, *The Shadow Box*, and *Heartbreak House*.

Open a new workbook and save it as Theater to the My Excel Files folders on your Student Disk. Plan and build a worksheet that tracks the sales of each of the four ticket types for all five of the plays. Calculate the total ticket sales for each play, the total sales for each of the four ticket types, and the total sales for all tickets.

Enter your own sales data, but assume the following: the Lightwell Players sold 800 tickets during the season; reserved seating was the most popular ticket type for all of the shows except for *The Shadow Box*; no play sold more than 10 student tickets. Plan and build a second worksheet in the workbook that reflects a 5% increase in sales of all ticket types.

To complete this independent challenge:

1 Think about the results you want to see, the information you need to build into these worksheets, and what types of calculations must be performed.

2 Sketch sample worksheets on a piece of paper to indicate how the information should be laid out. What information should go in the columns? In the rows?

3 Build the worksheets by entering a title, row labels, column headings, and formulas. Use named ranges to make the worksheet easier to use, and rename the sheet tabs to easily identify the contents of each sheet. (Hint: If your columns are too narrow, position the cell pointer in the column you want to widen. To widen the column, click Format on the menu bar, click Column, click Width, choose a new column width, and then click OK.)

4 Use separate worksheets for existing ticket sales and projected sales showing the 5% increase.

5 Save your work, then preview and print the worksheets.

6 Submit your sketches and printed worksheets.

INDEPENDENT
CHALLENGE 2

You have been promoted to computer lab manager at your school, and it is your responsibility to make sure there are enough computers for students during scheduled classes. Currently, you have four classrooms: three with IBM PCs and one with Macintoshes. Classes are scheduled Monday, Wednesday, and Friday in two-hour increments from 9 a.m. to 5 p.m. (the lab closes at 7 p.m.), and each room can currently accommodate 20 computers.

Open a new workbook and save it as Lab Manager to the My Excel Files folder on your Student Disk. Plan and build a worksheet that tracks the number of students who can currently use available computers per two-hour class. Create your enrollment data, but assume that current enrollment averages at 85% of each room's daily capacity. Using an additional worksheet, show the impact of an enrollment increase of 25%. To complete this independent challenge:

1 Think about how to construct these worksheets to create the desired output.

2 Sketch sample worksheets on a piece of paper, to indicate how the information should be laid out.

3 Build the worksheets by entering a title, row labels, column headings, and formulas. Use named ranges to make the worksheet easier to use, and rename the sheets to identify their contents easily.

4 Use separate sheets for actual enrollment and projected changes.

5 Save your work, then preview and print the worksheets.

6 Submit your sketches and printed worksheets.

INDEPENDENT
CHALLENGE 3

Nuts and Bolts is a small but growing hardware store that has hired you to organize its accounting records using Excel. The store hopes to track its inventory using Excel once its accounting records are under control. Before you were hired, one of the accounting staff started to enter expenses in a workbook, but the work was never completed.

Open the workbook XL 2-1 and save it as Nuts and Bolts finances in the My Excel Files folder on your Student Disk. Include functions such as the Average, Maximum, and Minimum amounts of each of the expenses in the worksheet.

To complete this independent challenge:

1 Think about what information would be important for the accounting staff to know.

2 Use the existing worksheet to create a paper sketch of the types of functions and formulas you will use and of where they will be located. Indicate where you will have named ranges.

3 Create your sketch using the existing worksheet as a foundation. Your worksheet should use range names in its formulas and functions.

4 Rename Sheet1 "Expenses."

5 Save your work, then preview and print the worksheet.

6 Submit your sketches and printed worksheets.

INDEPENDENT
CHALLENGE 4

You recently moved to a small town and joined the Chamber of Commerce. Since the other members are not computer-literate, you volunteered to organize the member organizations in a worksheet. The Chamber wants to use this information to keep track of members, as well as learn about types of industry in the community.

Fortunately, one of the other members started to enter the information but did not know how to complete it. The beginning work was saved in the file XL 2-2. Open this file and save it as Chamber members in the My Excel Files folder on your Student Disk. Membership dues are based on a member's revenue.

To complete this independent challenge:

1 Examine the information in the workbook on your Student Disk and think about how the Chamber could use it.

2 Sketch a sample worksheet on a piece of paper to indicate what information you would add and where it would be located.

3 Calculate each member's dues based on 1% of each member's revenue.

4 In another column, calculate each member's dues if that percentage were raised to 2%.

5 Rename the sheet to identify its contents easily.

6 Save your work, then preview and print the worksheet.

7 Submit your sketches and printed worksheet.

VISUALWORKSHOP

Create a worksheet similar to Figure 2-21 using the skills you learned in this unit. Save the workbook as Annual Budget to the My Excel Files folder on your Student Disk. Preview, then print the worksheet.

FIGURE 2-21: Visual Workshop

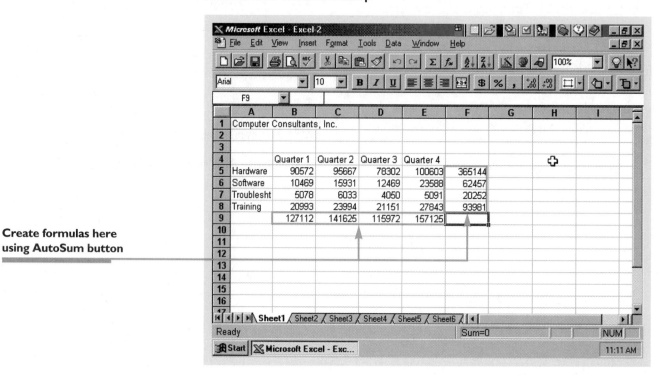

Create formulas here using AutoSum button

UNIT 3

Modifying
A WORKSHEET

ow you will learn how to insert and delete columns and rows; move, copy, paste, and format cell contents; and resize columns. **Case** The marketing managers at Nomad Ltd told Evan Brillstein that it would be helpful to have forecasts for the entire year, so Evan prepared a worksheet containing the forecast for the spring and fall tours sales and another worksheet with the forecast for the winter tours sales. He created these new worksheets as Sheet2 and Sheet3 in the workbook containing the 1996 Summer Tours Sales Forecast. Having three related worksheets in one workbook makes it easier for Evan to compare them. ▶

Opening an existing workbook

Sometimes it's useful to create a new worksheet by modifying one that already exists. This saves you from having to retype information. Throughout this book, you will be instructed to open a file from your Student Disk, use the Save As command to create a copy of the file with a new name, and then modify the new file by following the lesson steps. Saving the files with new names keeps your original Student Disk files intact in case you have to start the lesson over again or you wish to repeat an exercise. ▶** case** Follow along as Evan opens his 1996 Tours Forecast workbook, then uses the Save As command to create a copy with a new name.

STEPS

1 Start Excel then click the **Open button** 🗁 on the Standard toolbar
   The Open dialog box opens. See Figure 3-1. Notice that it is very similar to the Save As dialog box.

2 Click the **Look in list arrow**
   A list of the available drives appears. Locate the drive that contains your Student Disk. In these lessons we assume your Student Disk is in drive A.

3 Click 3½ **Floppy (A:)**
   A list of the files on your Student Disk appears in the Look in list box, with the default filename placeholder in the File name text box already selected.

4 In the File name list box, click **XL 3-1** then click **Open**
   The file XL 3-1 opens. You could also double-click the filename in the Look in list box to open the file. To create and save a copy of this file with a new name, Evan uses the Save As command.

5 Click **File** on the menu bar, then click·**Save As**
   The Save As dialog box opens.

6 Make sure the Save in list box displays the drive containing your Student Disk, then double-click **My Excel Files** in the list of folders
   You should save all your files to your Student Disk in the My Excel Files folder, unless instructed otherwise. If you do not have a My Excel Files folder, create one using the instructions in Saving a Workbook in Unit 2.

7 In the File name text box, select the current file name (if necessary), then type **Tour Info**
   See Figure 3-2.

8 Click **Save** to close the Save As dialog box, then click **OK** to close the Summary Info dialog box if necessary
   The file XL 3-1 closes, and a duplicate file named Tour Info is now open.

FIGURE 3-1: Open dialog box

Click to display a list of available drives

Available files and folders display here

The selected filename will appear here

FIGURE 3-2: Save As dialog box

Current folder

Type the new filename here

Your list of files might be different

TROUBLE?

All lessons from this point on assume you have Excel running. If you need help starting Excel, refer to Unit 1.■

Inserting and deleting rows and columns

As you modify a worksheet, you might find it necessary to insert or delete rows and columns. For example, you might need to insert rows to accommodate new inventory products or remove a column of yearly totals that are no longer current. Inserting or deleting rows or columns can help to make your worksheet more attractive and readable. Inserting or deleting rows or columns can also cause problems with formulas that reference cells in that area. For information on how to avoid these problems, see the related topic "Using dummy columns and rows." **case** Evan has already improved the appearance of his worksheet by using the Bold button to format the column headings. Now he decides to insert a row between the worksheet title and the column labels. Evan also decides to discontinue using the data related to bus tours for the 1996 summer season because of slow sales in 1995, so he needs to delete the row containing bus tour information.

1 Double-click the **Sheet1 tab** then name it **Summer**
This will identify this sheet of the workbook.

2 Click cell **A5**, click **Insert** on the menu bar, then click **Cells**
The Insert dialog box opens. See Figure 3-3. You can choose to insert a column or a row, or you can shift the data in the cells in the active column right or in the active row down. Evan wants to insert a row to add some space between the title and column headings.

3 Click the **Entire Row radio button**, then click **OK**
A blank row is inserted between the title and the month labels. When you insert a new row, the contents of the worksheet shift down from the newly inserted row. When you insert a new column, the contents of the worksheet shift to the right from the point of the new column. Now Evan deletes the row containing information about bus sales. Because the formulas in row 12 use ranges whose **anchors** (cells used in the range address) are in row 10 (the bus sales row), he can't delete row 10 without having to change the formulas. To get around this problem, he clears the data from row 10, then he deletes the blank row 11 so the worksheet doesn't have two blank rows together.

4 Select the range **A10:E10**, containing the bus tour information

5 Click **Edit** on the menu bar, point to **Clear**, then click **All**
The data in the range A10:E10 disappears. Notice that the formula results in rows 12 and 14 are adjusted because of the deletion of bus tour sales. Now delete a blank row.

6 Click the **row 11 selector button** (the gray box containing the row number to the left of the worksheet)
All of row 11 is selected as shown in Figure 3-4.

7 Click **Edit** in the menu bar, then click **Delete**
Excel deletes row 11, and all rows below this shift up one row. Evan is satisfied with the appearance of his worksheet and decides to save the changes.

8 Click the **Save button** 🖫 on the Standard toolbar

FIGURE 3-3:
Insert dialog box

Click here to
insert row

FIGURE 3-4:
Worksheet with
row 11 selected

Inserted row

Row 11
selector button

Using dummy columns and rows

You use cell references and ranges in formulas. When you add or delete a column
or row within a range used in a formula, Excel automatically adjusts the formula to
reflect the change. However, when you add a column or row at the end of a range
used in a formula, you must modify the formula to reflect the additional column or
row. To eliminate having to edit the formula, you can include a dummy column and
dummy row within the range you use for that formula. A **dummy column** or
dummy row is a blank column or row included at the bottom of but within a
range, as shown in Figure 3-5. Then if you add another column or row to the end
of the range, the formula will automatically be modified to include the new data.

Formula with
dummy row

Rows included
in formula

Dummy row

FIGURE 3-5:
Formula with
dummy row

Copying and moving cell entries

Using the Cut, Copy, and Paste buttons or Excel's drag-and-drop feature, you can copy or move information from one cell or range in your worksheet to another. You can also cut, copy, and paste data from one worksheet to another. **case** Evan included the 1996 forecast for spring and fall tours sales in his Tour Info workbook. He already entered the spring report in Sheet2 and will finish entering the labels and data for the fall report. Using the Copy and Paste buttons and drag-and-drop, Evan copies information from the spring report to the fall report.

1 Double-click the **Sheet2 tab** then rename it **Spring-Fall**
First, Evan copies the labels identifying the types of tours from the spring report to the fall report. Don't worry if you can't see all of the labels. You will fix this later.

**Moving and
Copying Text**

2 Select the range **A4:A9** then click the **Copy button** on the Standard toolbar
The selected range (A4:A9) is copied to the **Clipboard**, a temporary storage file that holds all the selected information you copy or cut. For more information, be sure to view the CourseHelp for this lesson. The **Cut button** removes the selected information and places it on the Clipboard. To copy the contents of the Clipboard to a new location, you click a new cell and then use the Paste command.

3 Click cell **A13**, then click the **Paste button** on the Standard toolbar
The contents of the Clipboard are copied into the range A13:A18. When pasting the contents of the Clipboard into the worksheet, you need to specify only the first cell of the range where you want the copied selection to go. Next, Evan decides to use drag-and-drop to copy the Total label.

4 Click cell **E3**, then position the pointer on any edge of the cell until the pointer changes to .

5 While the pointer is ⬚, press and hold down **[Ctrl]**
The pointer changes to ⬚.

6 While still pressing **[Ctrl]**, press and hold the left mouse button, then drag the cell contents to cell **E12**
As you drag, an outline of the cell moves with the pointer, as shown in Figure 3-6. When you release the mouse button, the Total label appears in cell E12. Evan now decides to move the worksheet title over to the left. To use drag-and-drop to move data to a new cell without copying do not press [Ctrl].

7 Click cell **C1**, then position the mouse on the edge of the cell until it changes to ⬚, then drag the cell contents to **A1**
Evan enters fall sales data into the range B13:D16, as shown in Figure 3-7.

8 Using the information shown in Figure 3-7, enter the sales data for the fall tours into the range B13:D16
Compare your worksheet to Figure 3-7, then continue to the next lesson.

FIGURE 3-6: Using drag-and-drop to copy information

Cut button

Copy button

Paste button

Copied cell

Outline of copied cell

Drag-and-drop pointer

FIGURE 3-7: Worksheet with fall tours data entered

Viewing CourseHelp

The camera icon indicates there is a CourseHelp available for this lesson. CourseHelps are on-screen slide shows that bring difficult concepts to life. Your instructor received a CourseHelp disk and should have installed it on the machine you are using. To start CourseHelp, click the Start button, point to Programs, point to CourseHelp, then click Microsoft Excel Illustrated. In the main CourseHelp window, click the topic that corresponds to this lesson. Because CourseHelp runs in a separate window, you can start and view a movie even if you're in the middle of completing a lesson. Once the movie is finished, you can click the Excel program button on the taskbar and continue with the lessons, right where you left off. You can see a list of all the CourseHelps available with this book in the Preface. CourseHelp icons also appear in the table of contents.

TROUBLE?

When you drag-and-drop into occupied cells, you will be asked if you want to replace the existing cells. Click OK to replace the contents with the cell you are moving.■

Copying and moving formulas

Copying and moving formulas allows you to reuse formulas you've already created. Copying formulas, rather than retyping them, helps to prevent new typing errors. ▶ase Evan wants to copy from the spring tours report to the fall tours report the formulas that total the tours by type and by month.

1 Click cell **E4** then click the **Copy button** 📋 on the Standard toolbar
The formula for calculating the total number of spring bike tours is copied to the Clipboard. Notice that the formula in the formula bar appears as =SUM(B4:D4).

2 Click cell **E13** then click the **Paste button** 📋 on the Standard toolbar
The formula from cell E4 is copied into cell E13. A new result of 50 appears in E13. Notice in the formula bar that the cell references have changed, so that the range B13:D13 appears in the formula. Formulas in Excel contain relative cell references. A **relative cell reference** tells Excel to copy the formula to a new cell, but to substitute new cell references so that the relationship of the cells to the formula in its new location remains unchanged. In this case, Excel inserted cells D13, C13, and B13, the three cell references immediately to the left of E13.

Notice that the bottom right corner of the active cell contains a small square, called the **fill handle**. Evan uses the fill handle to copy the formula in cell E13 to cells E14, E15, and E16. You can also use the fill handle to copy labels. See the related topic "Filling ranges with a series of labels" for more information.

3 Position the pointer over the fill handle until it changes to +

4 Drag the fill handle to select the range **E13: E16**
See Figure 3-8.

5 Release the mouse button
Once you release the mouse button, the fill handle copies the formula from the active cell (E13) and pastes it into each cell of the selected range. Again, because the formula uses relative cell references, cells E14 through E16 correctly display the totals for raft and canoe, horse, and bus tours. Continue with Step 6 to complete the fall tours section of the worksheet.

FIGURE 3-8: Selected range using the fill handle

Formula in E13 will be
copied to E14:E16

Mouse pointer

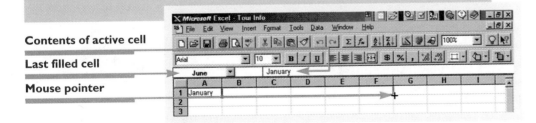

Filling ranges with a series of labels

You can fill cells with a series of labels using the fill handle. You can fill cells with sequential months, days of the week, years, and text plus a number (Quarter 1, Quarter 2, . . .). Figure 3-9 shows a series of months being created with the fill handle. As you drag the fill handle, the contents of the last filled cell appear in the name box. You can also use the Fill Series command on the Edit menu.

Contents of active cell

Last filled cell

Mouse pointer

FIGURE 3-9: Using the fill handle to create a label series

Copying and moving formulas, continued

If you need to make more than a few edits to a worksheet's labels and formulas, you can use the Replace command. See the related topic "Using Find and Replace to edit a worksheet" for more information. ▶case To complete the fall tours section of his worksheet, Evan now must copy the formulas from the range B9:E9 to the range B18:E18. To do this, he'll use the Copy and Paste commands and the Fill Right command.

6 Click cell **B9**, click **Edit** on the menu bar, then click **Copy**
The Copy command on the Edit menu has the same effect as clicking the Copy button 🖳 on the Standard toolbar. See Table 3-1 for Cut, Copy, Paste, and Undo shortcuts.

7 Click cell **B18**, click **Edit** on the menu bar, then click **Paste**
See Figure 3-10. The formula for calculating the September tours sales appears in the formula bar. You can also cut, copy, and paste among worksheets in a workbook. Now Evan uses the Fill Right command to copy the formula from cell B18 to cells C18, D18, and E18.

8 Select the range **B18:E18**

9 Click **Edit** on the menu bar, point to **Fill**, then click **Right**
The rest of the totals are filled in correctly. Compare your worksheet to Figure 3-11.

10 Click the **Save button** 🖫 on the Standard toolbar

TABLE 3-1: Cut, Copy, Paste, and Undo shortcuts

TOOL	KEYBOARD	MENU COMMAND	DESCRIPTION
✂	[Ctrl][X]	Edit Cut	Deletes the selection from the cell or range and places it on the Clipboard
🖳	[Ctrl][C]	Edit Copy	Copies the selection to the Clipboard
📋	[Ctrl][V]	Edit Paste	Pastes the contents of the Clipboard in the current cell or range
↩	[Ctrl][Z]	Edit Undo	Undoes the last editing action

FIGURE 3-10: Worksheet with copied formula

Copied formula
cell references

Copied formula result

	A	B	C	D	E	F	G	H	I
3	Spring	March	April	May	Total				
4	Bike	20	12	22	54				
5	Raft/Canoe	15	17	4	36				
6	Horse	30	36	23	89				
7	Bus	57	62	44	163				
8									
9	Total	122	127	93	342				
10									
11									
12	Fall	September	October	November	Total				
13	Bike	17	15	18	50				
14	Raft/Canoe	21	8	5	34				
15	Horse	12	21	14	47				
16	Bus	25	12	18	55				
17									
18	Total	75							

Cell reference B18 =SUM(B13:B16)

Select destination and press ENTER or choose Paste · Sum=75 · NUM

FIGURE 3-11:
Completed worksheet
with all formulas copied

	A	B	C	D	E
11					
12	Fall	September	October	November	Total
13	Bike	17	15	18	50
14	Raft/Canoe	21	8	5	34
15	Horse	12	21	14	47
16	Bus	25	12	18	55
17					
18	Total	75	56	55	186

Ready · Sum=372 · NUM

Using Find & Replace to edit a worksheet

If the worksheet is large and you need to make repeated changes to a worksheet's labels or formulas, use the Replace command on the Edit menu as a shortcut to locate and change the data more easily. The Replace dialog box is shown in Figure 3-12. Enter the text, values, or formulas you want to change, called the **search criteria**, in the Find What text box. In the Replace with text box, enter the text, values, or formulas that you want to replace the search criteria. Click Find Next to find the next occurrence of the search criteria, then click Replace to replace it with the replacement data, or click Replace All to replace all the instances of the search criteria in the workbook with the replacement data.

Type search
criteria here

Type replacement
data here

FIGURE 3-12: Replace dialog box

Copying formulas with absolute references

Relative v. Absolute Cell Referencing

Sometimes you might want a cell reference to always refer to a particular cell address. In such an instance, you would use an absolute cell reference. An **absolute cell reference** always refers to a specific cell address, even if you move the formula to a new location. You identify an absolute reference by placing a dollar sign ($) before the row letter and column number of the address (for example $A$1). Be sure to view the CourseHelp for this lesson before completing the steps. ▶**Case** Evan decides to add a column that calculates a possible increase in the number of spring tours in 1996. He wants to do a what-if analysis and recalculate the spreadsheet several times, changing the percentage that the tours might increase each time.

1 Click cell **G1**, type **Change**, then press **[→]**
Evan stores the increase factor that will be used in the what-if analysis in cell H1.

2 Type **1.1** in cell **H1**, then press **[Enter]**
This represents a 10% increase in sales.

3 Click cell **F3**, type **1997?**, then press **[Enter]**
Now, he creates a formula that uses an absolute reference to cell H1.

4 In cell **F4**, type **=E4*H1**, then click the **Enter button** ☑ on the formula bar
The result of 59.4 appears in cell F4. Evan now uses the fill handle to copy the formula in cell F4 to F5:F7.

5 Drag the fill handle to select the range **F4:F7**
The resulting values in the range F5:F7 are all zeros. When Evan looks at the formula in cell F5, which is =E5*H2, he realizes he needs to use an absolute reference to cell H1. Evan can correct this error by editing cell F4 using [F4], a shortcut key, to change the relative cell reference to an absolute cell reference.

6 Click cell **F4**, press **[2]** to change to Edit mode, then press **[F4]**
Dollar signs appear, changing the H1 cell reference to an absolute reference. See Figure 3-13.

7 Click the **Enter button** ☑ on the formula toolbar
Now that the formula correctly contains an absolute cell reference, Evan uses the fill handle to copy the formula in cell F4 to F5:F7.

8 Drag the fill handle to select the range **F4:F7**
Now Evan completes his what-if analysis by changing the value in cell H1 from 1.1 to 1.25 to indicate a 25% increase in sales.

9 Click cell **H1**, type **1.25**, then click the **Enter button** ☑ on the formula bar
The values in the range F4:F7 change. Compare your worksheet to Figure 3-14.

FIGURE 3-13: Absolute cell reference in cell F4

Absolute cell reference in formula

Incorrect values due to relative reference

FIGURE 3-14: Worksheet with what-if value

Absolute cell reference in formulas

QUICK **TIP**

Before you copy or move a formula, check to see if you need to use an absolute cell reference.■

Adjusting column widths

As you work with a worksheet, you might need to adjust the width of the columns to make your worksheet more usable. The default column width is 8.43 characters wide, a little less than one inch. With Excel, you can adjust the column width for one or more columns using the mouse or the Column command on the Format menu. Table 3-2 describes the commands available on the Format Column menu. You can also adjust the height of rows. See the related topic "Specifying row height" for more information. ▶**case**   Evan notices that some of the labels in column A and the fall month names don't fit in the cells. He decides to adjust the widths of columns A, B, C, and D so that the labels fit in the cells.

1   **Position the pointer on the column line between columns A and B**
The pointer changes to ┿, as shown in Figure 3-15. Evan makes the column wider.

2   **Drag the line to the right until column A is wide enough to accommodate all of the Raft/Canoe label**
Evan resizes the columns so they automatically accommodate the widest entry in a cell.

3   **Position the pointer on the column line between columns B and C until it changes to ┿, then double-click the left mouse button**
The width of column B is automatically resized to fit the widest entry, in this case, September. This feature is called **AutoFit**. You use the Column Width command on the Format menu to adjust several columns to the same width.

4   **Select the C, D, and E column selector buttons** (the gray boxes containing the column letters just above the worksheet)

5   **Click Format on the menu bar, point to Column, then click Width**
The Column Width dialog box appears. See Figure 3-16. Move the dialog box, if necessary, by dragging it by its title bar so you can see the contents of the worksheet.

6   **Type 10 in the Column Width text box, then click OK**
The column widths change to reflect the new settings. Evan is satisfied and decides to save his worksheet.

7   **Click the Save button 🖫 on the Standard toolbar**

TABLE 3-2: Format Column commands

COMMAND	DESCRIPTION
Width	Sets the width to a specific number of characters
AutoFit Selection	Fits the widest entry
Hide	Hide(s) column(s)
Unhide	Unhide(s) column(s)
Standard Width	Resets to default widths

FIGURE 3-15: Preparing to change the column width

Mouse pointer
between columns
A and B

FIGURE 3-16: Worksheet with Column Width dialog box

Selected columns

Type desired
width here

Specifying row height

The Row Height command on the Format menu allows you to customize row height
to improve readability. Row height is calculated in **points**, units of measure also
used for fonts—one inch equals 72 points. The row height must exceed the size of
the font you are using. For example, if you are using a 12 point font, the row height
must be more than 12 points. Normally, you don't need to adjust row heights manually. If you format something in a row to be a larger point size, Excel will adjust
the row to fit the largest point size in the row.

Formatting values

Formatting is how information appears in cells; it does not alter the data in any way. To format a cell, you select it, then apply the formatting you want. You can also format a range of cells. Cells and ranges can be formatted before or after data is entered. If you enter a value in a cell, and the cell appears to display the data incorrectly, you need to format the cell to display the value correctly. You might also want more than one cell to have the same format. For more information on how to do this, see the related topic, "Using the Format Painter."

▶case   The Marketing Department has also requested that Evan track tour advertising expenses. Evan developed a worksheet that tracks invoices for tour advertising. He formatted some of the values in the worksheet, and now he needs to finish.

1 Open the worksheet XL 3-2 from your Student Disk, then save it as Tour Ads in your My Excel Files folder
Refer to the lesson "Opening an existing worksheet" in this unit if you need help. First, Evan wants to format the data in the Cost ea. column so it displays with a dollar sign.

2 Select the range **E4:E32**, then click the **Currency button** ⬛ on the Formatting toolbar
Excel adds dollar signs and two decimal places to the Cost ea. column data. Columns G, H, and I contain dollar values also, but Evan doesn't want to repeat the dollar sign.

3 Select the range **G4:I32** then click the **Comma button** ⬛ on the Formatting toolbar
Column J contains percentages.

4 Select the range **J4:J32**, click the **Percentage button** ⬛ on the Formatting toolbar, then click the **Increase Decimal button** ⬛ to show one decimal place
Data in the % of Total column is changed. Now Evan reformats the invoice dates.

5 Select the range **B4:B31**, click **Format** on the menu bar, then click **Cells**
The Format Cells dialog box appears with the Number tab in front and the Date format already selected. See Figure 3-17. You can also use this dialog box to format ranges with currency, commas, and percentages.

6 Select the format **4-Mar-95** in the Type list box, then click **OK**
The selected dates change in appearance, but a series of pound signs (#####) displays because the dates no longer fit in the cells. Evan also notices that the totals in row 32 of columns E and G are too wide for their cells. He needs to use AutoFit to widen these columns.

7 Position the pointer between columns B and C until it changes to ↔, then double-click the **left mouse button**; then double-click the **left mouse button** when ↔ is between columns E and F and between columns G and H
Evan doesn't need the year to appear in the Inv Due column.

8 Select the range **C4:C31**, click **Format** on the menu bar, click **Cells**, click **4-Mar** in the Type list box, then click **OK**
Compare your worksheet to Figure 3-18. Now save the workbook.

9 Click the **Save button** ⬛ on the Standard toolbar.

FIGURE 3-17: Format Cells dialog box

Sample of
selected type

Select a category

Select a type

**FIGURE 3-18:
Worksheet with
formatted values**

Currency button

Percentage button

Comma button

Increase decimal
button

Decrease decimal
button

Modified date formats

Using the Format Painter

A cell's format can be "painted" into other cells using the Format Painter button ⟨ on the Formatting toolbar. This is similar to using drag-and-drop to copy information, but instead of copying cell contents, you copy only the cell format. Select the cell containing the desired format, then click ⟨. The pointer changes to ⊕⟨, as shown in Figure 3-19. Use this pointer to select the cell or range you want to contain the painted format.

Mouse painter

Destination of
painted format

Cell to be painted

**FIGURE 3-19: Using the
Format Painter**

TROUBLE?

If you don't see
EXCEL 3-2 in the
Look in list box in
the Open dialog
box, double-click
the letter of the
drive containing
your Student Disk
(probably drive A) in
the Look in list
area.∎

Changing fonts and point sizes

A **font** is the name given to a collection of characters (letters, numerals, symbols, and punctuation marks) with a specific design. The **point size** is the physical size of the text, measured in points. The default font in Excel is 10 point Arial. You can change the font, the size, or both of any entry or section in a worksheet by using the Format command on the menu bar or by using the Formatting toolbar. See the related topic, "Using the Formatting toolbar to change fonts and sizes" for more information on that method. Table 3-3 shows several fonts in different sizes. ▶**case** Evan wants to change the font and size of these labels to make the title and labels stand out.

1 Press **[Ctrl][Home]** to move to cell A1

2 Click **Format** on the menu bar, click **Cells**, then click the **Font tab**
See Figure 3-20. Evan decides to change the font of the title from Arial to Times New Roman, and he will increase the font size to 24.

3 Click **Times New Roman** in the Font list box, click **24** in the Size list box, then click **OK**
If you don't have Times New Roman in your list of fonts, choose another font. The title font appears in 24 point Times New Roman, and the Formatting toolbar displays the new font and size information. Next, Evan makes the column headings larger.

4 Select the range **A3:J3**, then click **Format** on the menu bar, then click **Cells**
The Font tab should still be the front-most tab.

5 Click **Times New Roman** in the Font list box, click **14** in the Size list box, then click **OK**

6 Resize the column widths in columns A through J so the larger labels fit in their cells
Compare your worksheet to Figure 3-21.

7 Click the **Save button** 🖫 on the Standard toolbar to save your formatting changes

TABLE 3-3: Types of fonts

FONT	12 POINT	24 POINT
Arial	Excel	Excel
Helvetica	Excel	Excel
Palatino	Excel	Excel
Times	Excel	Excel

FIGURE 3-20: Font tab of the Format Cells dialog box

Currently selected font

Available fonts on your computer

Effects options

Type a custom size or select from the list

Formatting attribute options

Sample of selected font

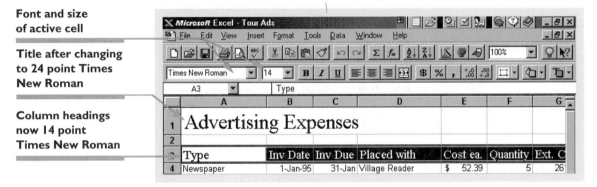

FIGURE 3-21: Worksheet with enlarged title and labels

Font and size of active cell

Title after changing to 24 point Times New Roman

Column headings now 14 point Times New Roman

Using the Formatting toolbar to change fonts and sizes

The font and size of the active cell appear on the Formatting toolbar. Click the Font list arrow, as shown in Figure 3-22, to see a list of available fonts. If you want to change the font, first select the text, click the Font list arrow, then choose the font you want. You can change the size of selected text in the same way, but click the Size list arrow to display a list of available point sizes.

Available fonts installed on your computer

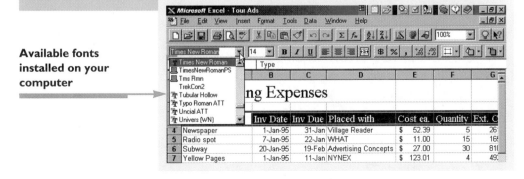

FIGURE 3-22: Available fonts on the Formatting toolbar

QUICK **TIP**

The Format cells dialog box displays a sample of the selected font. Use the Format Cells command if you're unsure of a font's appearance.■

Changing attributes and alignment

Attributes are styling features such as bold, italics, and underlining. You can apply bold, italics, and underlining from the Formatting toolbar or from the Font tab of the Format Cells dialog box. You can also change the alignment of text in cells. Left, right, or center alignment can be applied from the Formatting toolbar, or from the Alignment tab of the Format Cells dialog box. See Table 3-4 for a description of the available attribute and alignment buttons. Excel also has predefined worksheet formats to make formatting easier; see the related topic "Using AutoFormat" for more information. ▶case   Evan wants to further refine his worksheet by adding bold and underline formatting and centering some of the labels.

1 Click cell **A1** to select the title **Advertising Expenses**, then click the **Bold button** on the Formatting toolbar
The title Advertising Expenses appears in bold.

2 Select the range **A3:J3**, then click the **Underline button** on the Formatting toolbar
Excel underlines the column headings in the selected range.

3 Click cell **A3**, click the **Italics button** on the Formatting toolbar, then click
The word "Type" appears in boldface italic type. Notice that the Bold, Italics, and Underline buttons are indented. Evan decides he doesn't like the italic formatting. He removes it by clicking again.

4 Click
Excel removes italics from cell A3.

5 Add bold formatting to the rest of the labels in the range **B3:J3**
Evan wants to center the title over the data.

6 Select the range **A1:F1**, then click the **Center Across Columns button** on the Formatting toolbar
The title Advertising Expenses is centered across six columns. Now Evan centers the column headings in their cells.

7 Select the range **A3:J3** then click the **Center button** on the Formatting toolbar
Evan is satisfied with the formatting on this worksheet so he saves his changes.

8 Click the **Save button** on the Standard toolbar
Compare your screen to Figure 3-23. Highlighting information on a worksheet can be useful, but overuse of any attribute can be distracting and make a document less readable. Be consistent, adding emphasis the same way throughout a workbook.

9 Close the workbook, then exit Excel

FIGURE 3-23: Worksheet with formatting attributes applied

Center button

Tools indented

Column headings
centered, bold,
and underlines

Title centered
across columns

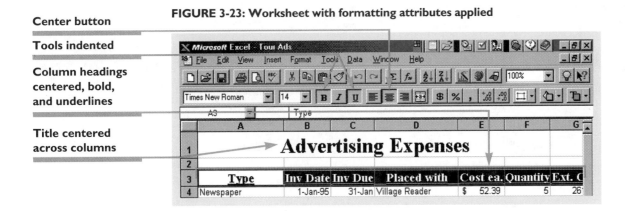

TABLE 3-4: Formatting buttons

ICON	DESCRIPTION	ICON	DESCRIPTION
B	Adds boldface		Aligns left
I	Italicizes		Aligns center
U	Underlines		Aligns right
	Adds lines or borders		Centers across columns

Using AutoFormat

Excel provides 16 preset formats called **AutoFormats**, which allow instant formatting of large amounts of data. AutoFormats are designed for worksheets with
labels in the left column and top rows and totals in the bottom row or right column. To use AutoFormatting, select the data to be formatted, click Format on the
menu bar, click AutoFormat, then select a format from the Table Format list box,
as shown in Figure 3-24.

List of AutoFormats

Sample of
selected format

FIGURE 3-24: AutoFormat dialog box

QUICK **TIP**

When selecting a
large, unnamed
range, select the
upper left-most cell
in the range, press
and hold [Shift],
then click the lower
right-most cell in the
range.■

TASKREFERENCE

TASK	MOUSE/BUTTON	MENU	KEYBOARD
Adjust column width	Double-click between columns	Click Format, Column, Width	
AutoFormat		Click Format, AutoFormat	
Bold attribute	**B**	Click Format, Cells, Font tab	[Ctrl][B]
Center across columns		Click Format, Cells, Alignment	
Center text		Click Format, Cells, Alignment	
Change font and point size	font list arrow & point list arrow	Click Format, Cells, Font tab	[Ctrl][1]
Comma format	,	Click Format, Cells, Number tab	[Ctrl][Shift][[!]
Copy cell entry		Click Edit, Copy	[Ctrl][C]
Currency format	**$**	Click Format, Cells, Number tab	[Ctrl][Shift][$]
Delete a row or column		Click column or row selector button, press [Delete]	[Ctrl][-]
Fill range with label series	Drag fill handle	Click Edit, Fill, Series	
Insert a row or column		Click column or row selector button, Insert, Cells	[Ctrl][+]
Italics attribute	*I*	Click Format, Cells, Font tab	[Ctrl][I]
Open a workbook		Click File, Open	[Ctrl][O]
Paint formats			
Paste cell entry		Click Edit, Paste	[Ctrl][V]
Underline attribute	U		[Ctrl][U]

CONCEPTSREVIEW

Label each of the elements of the Excel worksheet window shown in Figure 3-25.

1
2
3
4
5
6
7

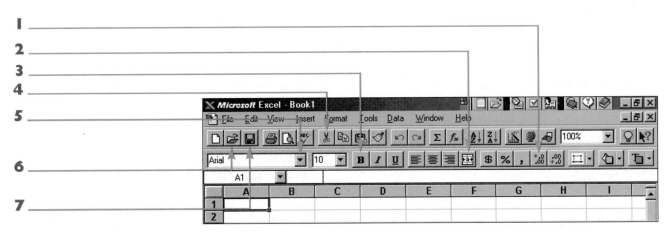

FIGURE 3-25

Match each of the statements to the command or button it describes.

8 Adds a new row or column

9 Erases the contents of a cell

10 Duplicates the contents of a cell

11 Changes the point size of selected cells

12 Pastes the contents of the Clipboard in the current cell

13 Changes the format to Currency

a. Format Cells

b. Edit Delete

c. Insert Row/Column

d. 📋

e. 💲

f. 📄

Select the best answer from the list of choices.

14 When you copy data using the Copy button, Excel puts the selected data on the

a. Border

b. Menu

c. Clipboard

d. Range

15 A cell address that changes when copied into a new location is called a(n)

a. Absolute reference

b. Relative reference

c. Mixed reference

d. Combined reference

16 Cell D4 contains the formula =A4+B4+C4. If you copy this formula to cell D5, what will the formula be in cell D5?

a. =$A$4+$B$4+$C$4

b. =A4+B4+C4-D4

c. =D5-D4

d. =A5+B5+C5

SKILLSREVIEW

1 Adjust column widths.

a. Open a new workbook.

b. Enter the information from Table 3-5 in your worksheet.

TABLE 3-5

Country Oak Chairs, Inc.

Quarterly Sales Sheet

Description	Price	Sold	Totals
Rocker	1299	1104	
Recliner	800	1805	
Bar stool	159	1098	
Dinette	369	1254	

c. Adjust all columns widths using the AutoFit feature.

d. Add a new sheet after the current sheet.

e. Delete the new sheet.

f. Save this workbook as Chairs in the My Excel Files folder on your Student Disk.

2 Format cell data with new fonts and point sizes.

a. Select the range of cells containing the column titles.

b. Change the font of the column titles to Times New Roman.

c. Increase the point size of the column titles to 14 point.

d. Resize columns as necessary.

e. Select the range of values in the Price column.

f. Click the Currency button.

g. Resize columns as necessary.

h. Save your workbook changes.

3 Copy and move formulas.

a. Enter the formula B4*C4 in cell D4. Adjust the number formatting, as needed.

b. Copy the formula in cell D4 to cells D5, D6, D7, and D8.

c. Adjust column widths as necessary.

d. Create a series of labels in A10:D10 for Quarter 1 through Quarter 4.

e. Use Replace to change "Oak" to "Maple."

f. Click the Undo button to change back to "Oak."

g. Save your workbook changes.

4 Format cell data with attributes and alignment.

a. Select the worksheet title Country Oak Chairs, Inc.

b. Click the Bold button to apply boldface to the title.

c. Select the label Quarterly Sales Sheet.

d. Click the Underline button to apply underlining to the label.

e. Select the range of cells containing the column titles.

f. Click the Align Center button to center the column titles.

g. Resize the column widths as necessary to fit the data.

h. Save your changes, then preview and print the workbook.

5 Insert a row.

a. Insert a new row between rows 4 and 5.

b. Add Country Oak Chairs' newest product—a Shaker bench in the newly inserted row. Enter "239" for the price and "360" for the number sold.

c. Use the fill handle to copy the formula in cell D4 to D5.

d. Save your changes, then preview and print the workbook.

e. Close the workbook.

6 Format values.

a. Open a new workbook.

b. Enter the information from Table 3-6 in your worksheet. Type "National Public Radio" contributions in cell A1, then type the values in the range A2:C7.

TABLE 3-6

National Public Radio contributions

City	Pledged	% Received
Honolulu	63000	.75
New York	42000	.63
San Francisco	45750	.54
Boston	52950	.52
Seattle	60000	.81

c. Use the Currency format to format the numbers in the Pledged column.

d. Create a new column, % Received, in D2:D7. This column calculates the actual amount received by NPR. (*Hint*: multiply column B by column C.)

e. Format the values in the % Received column using Currency.

f. Use the Percent format with no decimal places for the numbers in the % Received column.

g. Autofit columns B–D.

h. Change the width of the City column to 14 characters.

i. Make the worksheet title bold.

j. Save your workbook as "Natl Public Radio" in the My Excel Files folder on your Student Disk, then preview and print it.

k. Close the workbook.

7 Open an existing workbook.

a. Open the file XL 3-3 from your Student Disk.

b. Save it as "Recap" in the My Excel Files folder on your Student Disk.

c. Use the Bold button and Center button to format the column headings and row titles.

d. Increase the point size of the column headings in row 3 to 12 point.

e. Autofit the other columns.

e. Save your changes.

8 Copy formulas with absolute references.

a. Type "5.7%" in cell H3, then format this cell as a percentage with one decimal place.

b. Enter the formula F4*$H$3 in cell G4.

c. Copy the formula in cell G4 to G5:G9 using any method.

d. Save your changes then preview and print the workbook.

e. Close the workbook then exit Excel.

INDEPENDENT
CHALLENGE I

Write Brothers is a Houston-based company that manufactures high-quality pens and markers. As the finance manager, one of your responsibilities is to analyze the monthly reports from your five district sales offices. Your boss, Joanne Parker, has just told you to prepare a quarterly sales report for an upcoming meeting. Since several top executives will be attending this meeting, Joanne reminds you that the report must look professional. In particular, she asks you to emphasize the company's surge in profits during the last month and to highlight the fact that the Northeastern district continues to outpace the other districts.

Plan and build a worksheet that shows the company's sales during the last three months. Make sure you include:

- The number of pens sold (units sold) and the associated revenues (total sales) for each of the five district sales offices. The five Write Brothers sales districts include: Northeastern, Midwestern, Southeastern, Southern, and Western.

- Calculations that show month-by-month totals and a three-month cumulative total.

- Calculations that show each district's share of sales (percent of units sold).

- Formatting enhancements to emphasize the recent month's sales surge and the Northeastern district's sales leadership.

To complete this independent challenge:

1 Prepare a worksheet plan that states your goal, lists the worksheet data you'll need, and identifies the formulas for the different calculations.

2 Sketch a sample worksheet on a piece of paper, indicating how the information should be organized and formatted. How will you calculate the totals? What formulas can you copy to save time and keystrokes? Do any of these formulas need to use an absolute reference? How will you show dollar amounts? What information should be shown in bold? Do you need to use more than one font? More than one point size?

3 Build the worksheet with your own sales data. Enter the titles and labels first, then enter the numbers and formulas. Save the workbook as Write Brothers in the My Excel Files folder on your Student Disk.

4 Make enhancements to the worksheet. Adjust the column widths as necessary. Format labels and values, and change attributes and alignment.

5 Add a column that calculates a 10% increase in sales. Use an absolute cell reference in this calculation.

6 Before printing, preview the file so you know what the worksheet will look like. Adjust any items as needed, and print a copy. Save your work before closing the file.

7 Submit your worksheet plan, preliminary sketches, and the final printout.

INDEPENDENT
CHALLENGE 2

As the new computer lab manager of your class, you are responsible for all the computer equipment used in your classroom. In addition to knowing the current hardware and software capabilities and approximate capital costs, you must also be concerned with the number of hours the equipment is used, whether you would like to make any upgrades prior to the next semester, and those approximate costs. Plan and build a workbook that details the hardware and software used in your classroom. Make sure you include:

• The number of units and number of hours used

• Calculations that show the approximate value of hardware by unit and within the room

• The installed software and its total calculated value

• A "wish list" of hardware and software upgrades and their respective costs

• Formatting enhancements that emphasize the items of highest priority

To complete this independent challenge:

1 Prepare a worksheet plan that states your goal, lists the worksheet data you'll need, and identifies the formulas for the different calculations.

2 Sketch a sample worksheet on a piece of paper, indicating how the information should be formatted. What calculations are required? Can any of the formulas be copied? Do any of the formulas require an absolute reference? How will you make the numbers easy to read? What information should be shown in bold? Do you need to use more than one font? More than one point size?

3 Build the worksheet with the data you have gathered. Estimate the costs of hardware and software if you are unsure. Enter the titles and labels first, then enter the numbers and formulas. Save the workbook as Lab Costs in the My Excel Files folder on your Student Disk.

4 Make enhancements to the worksheet. Format labels and values, and change attributes and alignment.

5 Before printing, preview the file so you know what the worksheet will look like. Adjust any items as needed, and print a copy. Save your work before closing the file.

6 Submit your worksheet plan, preliminary sketches, and the final printout.

INDEPENDENT
CHALLENGE 3

Now that the Nuts and Bolts hardware store's accounting records are on Excel, they would like you to work on the inventory. Although more items will be added later, enough have been entered in a worksheet for you to begin your modifications.

Open the workbook XL 3-4 on your Student Disk, and save it as NB Inventory in the My Excel Files folder.

To complete this independent challenge:

1 Create a formula that calculates the Value of the inventory on-hand for each item.

2 Use an absolute reference to calculate the Sale Price of each item.

3 Use enhancements to make the title, column headings, and row headings more attractive.

4 Move the column containing the on-hand values so it displays to the left of the Sold by column.

5 Make sure all columns are wide enough to see the data.

6 Before printing, preview the file so you know what the worksheet will look like. Adjust any items as needed, and print a copy. Save your work before closing the file.

7 Submit your final printout.

INDEPENDENT
CHALLENGE 4

Continuing your efforts with the Chamber of Commerce, you need to examine the membership in comparison to the community more closely.

Open the workbook XL 3-5 on your Student Disk, and save it as Community in the My Excel Files folder.

To complete this independent challenge:

1 Remove any blank columns.

2 Format the Annual Revenue column using the Currency format.

3 Make all columns wide enough to fit their data.

4 Use formatting enhancements, such as fonts, font sizes, and text attributes, to make the worksheet more attractive.

5 Before printing, preview the file so you know what the worksheet will look like. Adjust any items as needed, and print a copy. Save your work before closing the file.

6 Submit your final printout.

VISUALWORKSHOP

Create the following worksheet using the skills you learned in this unit. Open the file XL 3-6 on your Student Disk, and save it as January Invoices in the My Excel Files folder. (*Hint*: The only additional font used in this exercise is Times New Roman. It is 22 points in row 1, and 14 points in row 3.)

FIGURE 3-26: Visual Workshop

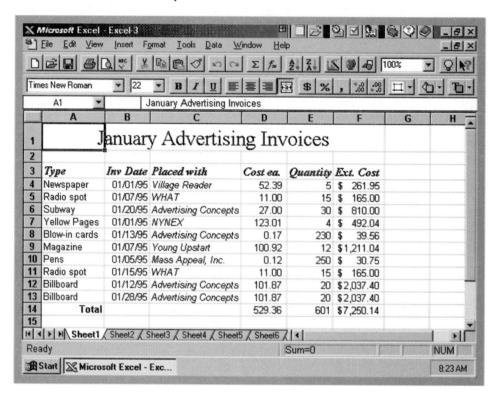

UNIT 4

OBJECTIVES

▶ Plan and design a chart

▶ Create a chart

▶ Edit a chart

▶ Move and resize a chart and its objects

▶ Change the appearance of a chart

▶ Enhance a chart

▶ Add text annotations and arrows to a chart

▶ Preview and print a chart

Working
WITH CHARTS

Worksheets provide an effective way to organize information, but they are not always the best format for presenting data to others. Information in a selected range or worksheet can be easily converted to the visual format of a chart. Charts quickly communicate the relationships of data in a worksheet. In this unit, you will learn how to create a chart, edit a chart and change the chart type, add text annotations and arrows to a chart, then preview and print it. **case** Evan Brillstein needs to create a chart showing the six-month sales history at Nomad Ltd for the annual meeting. He wants to illustrate the impact of an advertising campaign that started in June. ▶

Planning and designing a chart

**Choosing a
Chart Type**

Before creating a chart, you need to plan what you want your chart to show and how you want it to look. Be sure to view the CourseHelp for this lesson before completing the steps. ▶**case** Evan wants to create a chart to be used at the annual meeting. The chart will show the spring and summer sales throughout the Nomad Ltd regions. In early June, the Marketing Department launched a national advertising campaign. The results of the campaign were increased sales for the summer months. Evan wants his chart to illustrate this dramatic sales increase. ▶ Evan uses the worksheet shown in Figure 4-1 and the following guidelines to plan the chart:

1 **Determine the purpose of the chart, and identify the data relationships you want to communicate visually**
Evan wants to create a chart that shows sales throughout Nomad's regions in the spring and summer months (March through August). He particularly wants to highlight the increase in sales that occurred in the summer months as a result of the advertising campaign.

2 **Determine the results you want to see, and decide which chart type is most appropriate to use; Table 4-1 describes several different types of charts**
Because he wants to compare related data (sales in each of the regions) over a time period (the months March through August), Evan decides to use a column chart.

3 **Identify the worksheet data you want the chart to illustrate**
Evan is using data from his worksheet titled "Nomad Ltd Regions, Spring and Summer Sales," as shown in Figure 4-1. This worksheet contains the sales data for the five regions from March through August.

4 **Sketch the chart, then use this sketch to decide where the chart elements should be placed**
Evan sketches his chart as shown in Figure 4-2. He puts the months on the horizontal axis (the **x-axis**) and the monthly sales figures on the vertical axis (the **y-axis**). The **tick marks** on the y-axis create a scale of measure for each value. Each value in a cell he selects for his chart is a **data point**. In any chart, each data point is visually represented by a **data marker**, which in this case is a column. A collection of related data points is a **data series**. In Evan's chart, there are five data series (Midwest, Northeast, Northwest, South, and Southwest) so he has included a **legend** to identify them.

FIGURE 4-1: Worksheet containing sales data

FIGURE 4-2: Evan's sketch of the column chart

TABLE 4-1: Commonly used chart types

TYPE	BUTTON	DESCRIPTION
Area		Shows how volume changes over time
Bar		Compares distinct, unrelated objects over time using a horizontal format; sometimes referred to as a horizontal bar chart in other spreadsheet programs
Column		Compares distinct, unrelated objects over time using a vertical format; the Excel default; sometimes referred to as a bar chart in other spreadsheet programs
Line		Compares trends over even time intervals; similar to an area chart
Pie		Compares sizes of pieces as part of a whole; can have slices pulled away from the pie, or "exploded"
XY (scatter)		Compares trends over uneven time or measurement intervals; used in scientific and engineering disciplines for trend spotting and extrapolation
Combination	none	Combines a column and line chart to compare data requiring different scales of measure

Creating a chart

To create a chart in Excel, you first select the range containing the data you want to chart. Once you've selected a range, you can use Excel's ChartWizard to lead you through the chart creation process. ▶**ase** Using the worksheet containing the spring and summer sales data for the five regions, Evan will create a chart that shows the monthly sales of each region from March through August.

1 **Open the workbook XL 4-1 from your Student Disk, then save it as Nomad Regions to the My Excel Files folder**
First, Evan needs to select the cells he wants to chart. He wants to include the monthly sales figures for each of the regions, but not the totals. He also wants to include the month and region labels.

2 **Select the range A5:G10, then click the ChartWizard button** on the Standard toolbar
When you click the ChartWizard button, the pointer changes to $^+$. See Figure 4-3. This pointer draws the border of the chart. Evan decides to place the chart directly below the worksheet.

3 **Position $^+$ so that the cross is at the top of cell A13, as shown in Figure 4-3, then drag the pointer to the lower-right corner of cell H24 to select the range A13:H24**
The first of five ChartWizard dialog boxes opens. This box confirms the range of data to be charted.

4 **Make sure the range is the same as the one you selected in Step 3, then click Next**
The second ChartWizard dialog box lets you choose the type of chart you want to create.

5 **Click Next to accept the default chart type of column**
The third dialog box lets you choose the format of the chart. Evan wants each region to have a different color bar, so he again accepts the default choice.

6 **Click Next**
The fourth ChartWizard dialog box shows a sample chart using the data you selected. Notice that the regions (the rows in the selected range) are plotted according to the months (the columns in the selected range), and that the months were added as labels for each data series. You could switch this by clicking the Columns radio button below Data Series on the right side of the dialog box. Notice also that there is a legend showing each region and its corresponding color on the chart.

7 **Click Next**
In the last ChartWizard dialog box, you can choose to keep the legend, add a chart title, and add axis titles. Evan adds a title.

8 **Click in the Chart Title text box, then type Nomad Ltd Regional Sales**
After a moment, the title appears in the Sample Chart box. See Figure 4-4.

9 **Click Finish**
The column chart appears in the defined plot area, as shown in Figure 4-5. Your chart might look slightly different. Just as Evan had hoped, the chart shows the dramatic increase in sales between May and June. The **selection handles**, the small black squares at the corners and sides of the chart's border, indicate that the chart is selected. Anytime a chart is selected (as it is now), the Chart toolbar appears. It might be floating, as shown in Figure 4-5, or it might be fixed at the top of the worksheet window.

FIGURE 4-3: Worksheet with selected range and ChartWizard pointer

ChartWizard button depressed

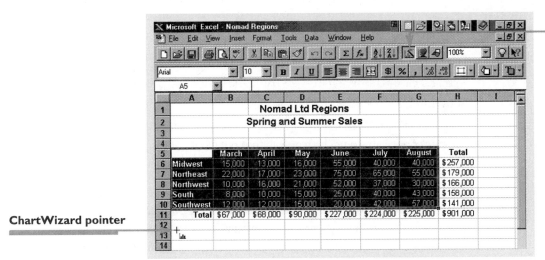

ChartWizard pointer

FIGURE 4-4: Completed ChartWizard dialog box

Title added

Miniaturized chart

Legend

Radio buttons for displaying legend

FIGURE 4-5: Worksheet with column chart

Floating chart toolbar

Selection handles

Title

Legend

Month labels on x-axis

TROUBLE?

If you want to delete a chart, select it then press [Delete].

Editing a chart

Once you've created a chart, it's easy to modify it. You can change data values in the worksheet, and the chart will automatically be updated to reflect the new data. You can also easily change chart types using the buttons on the Chart toolbar. Table 4-2 shows and describes the Chart toolbar buttons. ▶case Evan looks over his worksheet and realizes he entered the wrong data for the Northwest region in July and August. After he corrects this data, he wants to find out what percentage of total sales the month of June represents. He will convert the column chart to a pie chart to find this out.

1 **Scroll the worksheet so that you can see both the chart and row 8, containing the Northwest region's sales figures, at the same time**
As you enter the correct values, watch the columns for July and August in the chart change.

2 **Click cell F8, type 49000 to correct the July sales figure, press [RightArrow], type 45000 in cell G8, then press [Enter]**
The Northwest columns for July and August reflect the increased sales figures. See Figure 4-6.

3 **Select the chart by clicking anywhere within the chart border, then click the Chart Type list arrow on the Chart toolbar**
The chart type buttons appear, as shown in Figure 4-7.

4 **Click the 2-D Pie Chart button** ⊙
The column chart changes to a pie chart showing total sales by month (the columns in the selected range). See Figure 4-8. Evan looks at the pie chart, takes some notes, and then decides to convert it back to a column chart. Evan now wants to see if the large increase in sales would be better presented with a three-dimensional column chart.

5 **Click the Chart Type list arrow on the Chart toolbar, then click the 3-D Column Chart button** 🗠
A three-dimensional column chart appears. Evan could rotate the chart for a better view. See the related topic "Rotating a chart" for more information. Evan notes that the three-dimensional column format is too crowded, so he switches back to the two-dimensional format.

6 **Click the Chart Type list arrow on the Chart toolbar, then click the 2-D Column Chart button** 📊

7 **Click the Save button** 💾 **on the Standard toolbar**

TABLE 4-2: Chart type buttons

BUTTON	DESCRIPTION	BUTTON	DESCRIPTION
📈	Displays 2-D area chart	📐	Displays 3-D area chart
📊	Displays 2-D bar chart	📚	Displays 3-D bar chart
📊	Displays 2-D column chart	📊	Displays 3-D column chart
📉	Displays 2-D line chart	📉	Displays 3-D line chart
⊙	Displays 2-D pie chart	🥧	Displays 3-D pie chart
🔲	Displays 2-D scatter chart	📦	Displays 3-D surface chart
⊙	Displays 2-D doughnut chart	⭐	Displays radar chart

FIGURE 4-6:
Worksheet with new
data entered for the
Northwest region

Adjusted data points

New data

	A	B	C	D	E	F	G	H	I
8	Northwest	10,000	16,000	21,000	52,000	49,000	45,000	$193,000	
9	South	8,000	10,000	15,000	25,000	40,000	43,000	$158,000	
10	Southwest	12,000	12,000	15,000	20,000	42,000	57,000	$141,000	
11	Total	$67,000	$68,000	$90,000	$227,000	$236,000	$240,000	$928,000	

Nomad Ltd Regional Sales

Midwest · Northeast · Northwest · South · Southwest

March April May June July August

Sheet1 / Sheet2 / Sheet3 / Sheet4 / Sheet5 / Sheet6

Ready   Sum= 43,000   NUM

Start | Microsoft Excel - No...   8:45 AM

FIGURE 4-7:
Chart Type list box

3-D Column Chart
button

2-D Column Chart
button

2-D Pie Chart button

FIGURE 4-8: Pie chart

Nomad Ltd Regional Sales

March · April · May · June · July · August

June sales pie slice

Sheet1 / Sheet2 / Sheet3 / Sheet4 / Sheet5 / Sheet6

Double-click chart to edit   NUM

Start | Microsoft Excel - No...   8:46 AM

Rotating a chart

In a three-dimensional chart, columns or bars can sometimes be obscured by
other data series within the same chart. You can rotate the chart until a better view
is obtained. Double-click the chart, click the tip of one of its axes, then drag the
handles until a more pleasing view of the data series appears. See Figure 4-9.

FIGURE 4-9:
3-D chart rotated with
improved view of data
series

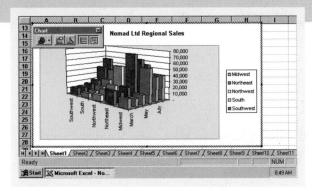

Nomad Ltd Regional Sales

Midwest · Northeast · Northwest · South · Southwest

Southwest · South · Northwest · Northeast · Midwest · March · May · July

Sheet1 / Sheet2 / Sheet3 / Sheet4 / Sheet5 / Sheet6 / Sheet7 / Sheet8 / Sheet9 / Sheet10 / Sheet11

Ready   NUM

Start | Microsoft Excel - No...   8:49 AM

Moving and resizing a chart and its objects

Charts are graphics, or drawn **objects**, and have no specific cell or range address. You can move charts anywhere on a worksheet without affecting formulas or data in the worksheet. You can even put them on another sheet. See the related topic "Viewing multiple worksheets" for more information. You can also easily resize a chart to improve its appearance by dragging the selection handles. Drawn objects such as charts can contain other objects that you can move and resize. To move an object, select it then drag it or cut and copy it to a new location. To resize an object, use the selection handles. **case** Evan wants to increase the size of the chart and center it on the worksheet. He also wants to move the legend up so that it is level with the title.

1 Select the **chart**, scroll the worksheet until row 28 is visible, then position the pointer over the bottom center selection handle until the pointer changes to ↕
The pointer shape ↕ indicates that you can use a selection handle to resize the chart.

2 Press and hold the mouse button, drag the lower edge of the chart to row 28, then release the mouse button
A dotted outline of the chart perimeter appears as the chart is being resized, and the pointer changes to ┼. The chart length is increased.

3 Position the pointer over one of the selection handles on the right, then drag the right edge of the chart about ½" to the right to the middle of column I
See Figure 4-10. Now, Evan moves the legend up so that it is level with the chart title.

4 Double-click the **chart**
The chart is now in Edit mode. When the chart is in **Edit mode**, you can move and edit objects within the chart border. When the chart is selected but not in Edit mode, you can move and resize the entire chart. In Edit mode, the chart appears in its own window, and the menu bar changes to the Chart menu bar.

5 Click the **legend** to select it, then drag it to the upper-right corner of the chart until it is aligned with the chart title
If the Chart toolbar is in the way of the legend, move it out of your way first. Selection handles appear around the legend when you click it, and a dotted outline of the legend perimeter appears as you drag. See Figure 4-11.

6 Press **[Esc]** to deselect the legend

7 Click the **Save button** 🖫 on the Standard toolbar

FIGURE 4-10:
Worksheet with
resized and centered
chart

Lengthened to row 28

Widened to column I

FIGURE 4-11:
Worksheet with
repositioned legend

Chart menu bar

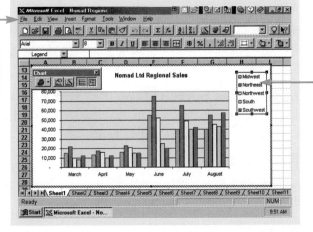

Repositioned legend

Viewing multiple worksheets

A workbook can be organized with a chart on one sheet and the data on another
sheet. With this organization, you can still see the data next to the chart by opening
multiple windows of the same workbook. This allows you to see portions of multiple sheets at the same time. Click Window on the menu bar, then click New
Window. A new window containing the current workbook opens. To see the windows next to each other, click Window on the menu bar, click Arrange, then
choose one of the options in the Arrange Windows dialog box. You can open one
worksheet in one window and a different worksheet in the second window. See
Figure 4-12. To close one window without closing the worksheet, double-click the
control menu box on the window you want to close.

FIGURE 4-12:
Workbook with
two windows open

Individual title bars

Active sheet tabs

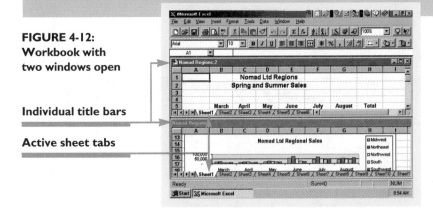

Changing the appearance of a chart

After you've created a chart using the ChartWizard, you can modify its appearance by changing the colors of data series and adding or eliminating a legend and gridlines using the Chart toolbar. **Gridlines** are the horizontal lines in the chart that enable the eye to follow the value on an axis. The corresponding Chart toolbar buttons are listed in Table 4-3. **case** Evan wants to make some changes in the appearance of his chart. He wants to see if the chart looks better without gridlines, and he wants to change the color of a data series.

1 **Make sure the chart is still in Edit mode**
Evan wants to see how the chart looks without gridlines. Currently gridlines appear and the Gridlines button on the Chart toolbar is depressed.

2 **Click the Gridlines button on the Chart toolbar**
The gridlines disappear from the chart, and the button is deselected. Evan decides that the gridlines are necessary to the chart's readability.

3 **Click again**
The gridlines reappear. Evan is not happy with the color of the columns for the South data series and would like the columns to stand out more.

4 **With the chart in Edit mode, double-click any column in the South data series**
Handles appear on all the columns in the series, and the Format Data Series dialog box opens, as shown in Figure 4-13. Make sure the Patterns tab is the front-most tab.

5 **Click the green box (in the first row, fourth from the left), then click OK**
All the columns in the series are green. Compare your finished chart to Figure 4-14. Evan is pleased with the change.

6 **Click the Save button on the Standard toolbar**

TABLE 4-3: Chart enhancement buttons

BUTTON	USE
	Adds or deletes gridlines
	Adds or deletes legend
	Returns you to the ChartWizard

FIGURE 4-13: Format Data Series dialog box

Sample of selected color

FIGURE 4-14: Chart with formatted data series

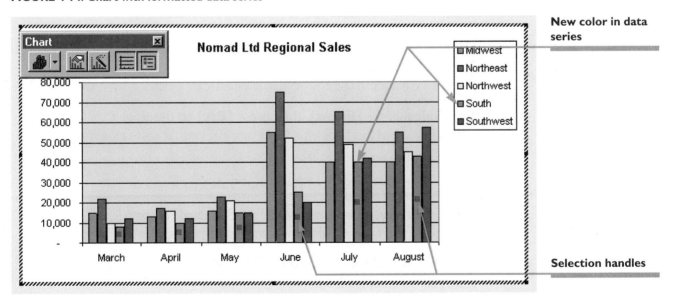

New color in data series

Selection handles

QUICK **TIP**

Experiment with different formats for your charts until you get just the right look.■

Enhancing a chart

There are many ways to enhance a chart to make it easier to read and understand. You can create titles for the x-axis and y-axis, add graphics, or add background color. You can even format the text you use in a chart. See the related topic "Changing text font and alignment in charts" for more information. ▶case Evan wants to improve the appearance of his chart by creating titles for the x-axis and y-axis. He also decides to add a drop shadow to the title.

1 Double-click the chart to make sure it is in Edit mode
   Evan wants to add descriptive text to the x-axis.

2 Click **Insert** on the Chart menu bar, click **Titles**, click the **Category (X) Axis check box**, then click **OK**
   A text box with selection handles around it and containing an "X" appears below the x-axis, as shown in Figure 4-15.

3 Type **Months**, then click the **Enter button** 🔲 on the formula bar
   The word "Months" appears below the month labels. If you wanted to move the axis title to a new position, you could click on an edge of the selection and drag it. If you wanted to edit the axis title, position the pointer over the selected text box until it becomes I and click, then edit the text. Evan now adds text to the y-axis.

4 Click **Insert** on the Chart menu bar, click **Titles**, click the **Value (Y) Series check box**, then click **OK**
   A selected text box containing a "Y" appears to the left of the y-axis.

5 Type **Sales**, press **[Enter]**, then press **[Esc]** to deselect it
   The word "Sales" appears to the left of the regions. Next Evan decides to add a drop shadow to the title.

6 Click the title **Nomad Ltd Regional Sales** to select it

7 Click the **Drawing button** 🔲 on the Standard toolbar
   The Drawing toolbar appears. If the Drawing toolbar is in the way, move it by dragging its title bar.

8 Click the **Drop Shadow button** 🔲 on the Drawing toolbar, then press **[Esc]** to deselect the title
   A drop shadow appears around the title. See Figure 4-16.

9 Click the **Drawing button** 🔲 then click the **Save button** 🔲 on the Standard toolbar
   The Drawing toolbar no longer appears, and the chart is saved.

FIGURE 4-15: Chart with selected text box

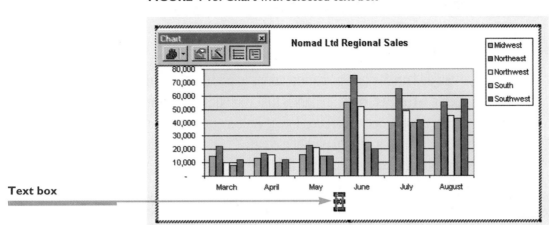

Text box

FIGURE 4-16: Enhanced chart

Drop shadow added

Y-axis title

Drawing toolbar

X-axis title

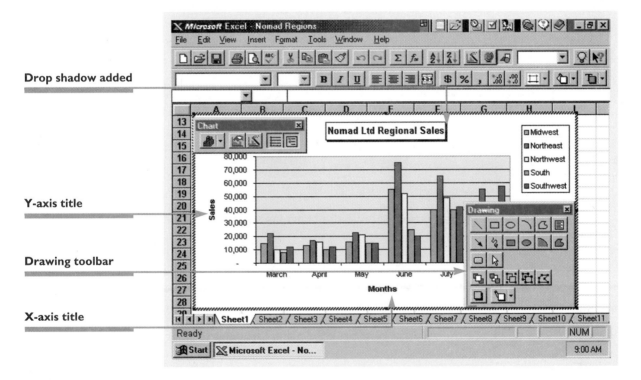

Changing text font and alignment in charts

The font and the alignment of axis text can be modified to make it more readable or to better fit within the plot area. With a chart in Edit mode, double-click the text to be modified. The Format Axis dialog box appears. Click the Font or the Alignment tab, make the desired changes, then click OK.

Adding text annotations and arrows to a chart

You can add arrows and text annotations to highlight information in your charts. **Text annotations** are labels that you add to a chart to draw attention to a certain part of it. See the related topic "Pulling out a pie slice" for another way to draw attention to a certain part of a chart. ▶**case** Evan wants to add a text annotation and an arrow to highlight the June sales increase.

1 Make sure the chart is in Edit mode
   Evan wants to call attention to the June sales increase by drawing an arrow that points to the top of the June data series with the annotation, "After advertising campaign." To enter the text for an annotation, you simply start typing.

2 Type **After advertising campaign** then click the **Enter button** ☑ on the formula bar
   As you type, the text appears in the formula bar. After you confirm the entry, the text appears in a selected text box within the chart window. See Figure 4-17. Your text box might be in a different location on your screen.

3 Point to an edge of the text box, then press and hold the **left mouse button**
   The pointer should be ⌖, and the message in the status bar should say "Move selected objects." If the pointer changes to I or ↔, release the mouse button, click outside the text box area to deselect it, then select the text box and repeat Step 3.

4 Drag the text box above the chart, as shown in Figure 4-18, then release the mouse button
   Evan is ready to add an arrow.

5 Click the **Drawing button** ▣ on the Standard toolbar
   The Drawing toolbar appears.

6 Click the **Arrow button** ◨ on the Drawing toolbar
   The pointer changes to ＋.

7 Position ＋ under the word "campaign" in the text box, click the **left mouse button**, drag the line to the June sales, then release the mouse button
   An arrowhead appears pointing to the June sales. Compare your finished chart to Figure 4-18.

8 Close the Drawing toolbar, then click the **Save button** 🖫 on the Standard toolbar

FIGURE 4-17: Chart with new text box

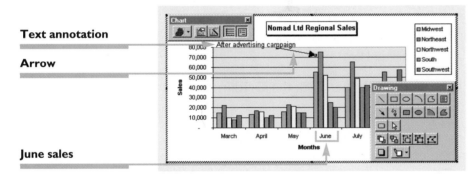

Drawing button

Move text box here

Selected floating text box

FIGURE 4-18: Completed chart with text annotation and arrow

Text annotation

Arrow

June sales

Pulling out a pie slice

Just as an arrow can call attention to a data series, you can emphasize a pie slice by **exploding** it, or pulling it away from, the pie chart. Once the chart is in Edit mode, click the pie to select it, click the desired slice to select only the slice, then drag the slice away from the pie, as shown in Figure 4-19. After you change the chart type, you may need to adjust arrows within the chart.

Slice pulled from pie

FIGURE 4-19: Exploded pie slice

QUICK **TIP**

You can insert text and an arrow in the data section of a worksheet by clicking the Text Box button 🗐 on the Standard toolbar, drawing a text box, typing the text, and then adding the arrow.■

Previewing and printing a chart

After you complete a chart to your satisfaction, you will need to print it. You can print a chart by itself, or as part of the worksheet. ▶**case** Evan is satisfied with the chart and wants to print it for the annual meeting. He will print the worksheet and the chart together, so that the shareholders can see the actual sales numbers for each tour type.

1. Click in any cell outside the chart to turn off Edit mode, then click outside the chart to deselect it
   If you wanted to print only the chart without the data, you would leave the chart in Edit mode.

2. Click the **Print Preview button** 🔍 on the Standard toolbar
   The Print Preview window opens. Evan decides that the chart and data would look better if they were printed in **landscape** orientation—that is, with the page turned sideways. To change the orientation of the page, you must alter the page setup.

3. Click **Setup** to display the Page Setup dialog box, then click the **Page tab**

4. Click the **Landscape radio button** in the Orientation section
   See Figure 4-20. Evan would also like to eliminate the gridlines that appear in the data to give the page a more finished look.

5. Click the **Sheet tab** then click the **Gridlines check box** to deselect it
   The chart and data will print too far over to the left of the page. Evan changes this using the Margins tab.

6. Click the **Margins tab**, double-click the Left text box, type **2.25**, then click **OK**
   The print preview of the worksheet appears again. The data and chart are centered on the page that is turned sideways, and no gridlines appear. See Figure 4-21. Evan is satisfied with the way it looks and prints it.

7. Click **Print** to display the Print dialog box, then click **OK**
   Your printed report should look like the image displayed in the Print Preview window.

8. Click the **Save button** 💾 on the Standard toolbar, click **File** on the menu bar, then click **Close**
   Your workbook closes.

9. Click **File** on the menu bar, then click **Exit** to exit Excel and return to the desktop

FIGURE 4-20: Page tab of the Page Setup dialog box

Landscape selected

FIGURE 4-21: Chart and data ready to print

Gridlines off

Orientation changed
to landscape

Centered on page

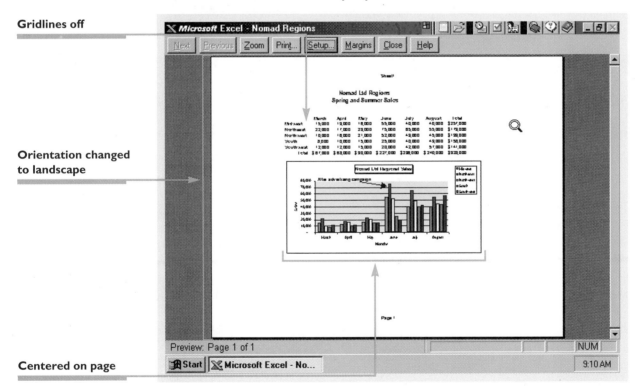

QUICK **TIP**

You can print charts
and worksheets on
transparencies for
use on an overhead
projector.■

TASKREFERENCE

TASK	MOUSE/BUTTON	MENU	KEYBOARD
Add arrow			
Add drop shadow			
Add gridlines to chart in Edit mode		Click Insert, Gridlines	[Alt][I][G]
Add title to chart in Edit mode		Click Insert, Titles	[Alt][I][T]
Change type of chart in Edit mode		Click Format, Chart Type	[Alt][O][T]
Change type of selected chart			
Chart in Edit mode	Double-click chart		
Create an embedded chart		Click Insert, Chart, On This Sheet	[Alt][I][H][O]
Delete a selected chart			[Delete]
Deselect a chart	Click outside chart		[Esc]
Edit data series color of chart in Edit mode	Double-click data series, select color in Patterns tab, click OK	Click Format, Selected Data Series, select color in Patterns tab, click OK	[Alt][O][E]
Explode pie slice of chart in Edit mode	Click pie, click slice, drag slice from pie		
Move/resize a chart	Drag handle to new location		
Open Drawing toolbar			
Preview chart		Click File, Print Preview	[Alt][F][V]
Print chart		Click File, Print	[Ctrl][P]
Rotate chart in Edit mode	Click axes, drag handles		
Select a chart	Click chart		

CONCEPTSREVIEW

Label each of the elements of the Excel chart shown in Figure 4-22.

1 _____

2 _____

3 _____

4 _____

5 _____

6 _____

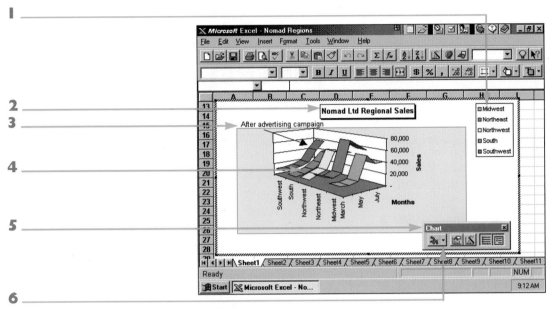

FIGURE 4-22

Match each of the statements with its chart type.

7 Shows how volume changes over time

8 Compares data as parts of a whole

9 Displays a column and line chart using different scales of measurement

10 Compares trends over even time intervals

11 Compares data over time—the Excel default

a. Column
b. Area
c. Pie
d. Combination
e. Line

Select the best answer from the list of choices.

12 The box that identifies patterns used for each data series is a
   a. Data point
   b. Plot
   c. Legend
   d. Range

13 What is the term for a row or column on a chart?
   a. Range address
   b. Axis title
   c. Chart orientation
   d. Data series

SKILLSREVIEW

1 Create a distribution report worksheet, then create a column chart.
   a. Start Excel, open a new workbook, then save it as Software Used to the My Excel Files folder on your Student Disk.
   b. Enter the information from Table 4-4 in your worksheet in range A1:E6. Resize columns and rows.

TABLE 4-4

	Excel	Word	WordPerfect	PageMaker
Accounting	10	1	9	0
Marketing	2	9	0	6
Engineering	12	5	7	1
Personnel	2	2	2	1
Production	6	3	4	0

   c. Save your work.
   d. Select all the entered information, then click the ChartWizard button.
   e. Select the range you want to chart.
   f. Complete the ChartWizard dialog boxes and build a two-dimensional column chart with a different color bar for each department and with the title "Software Distribution by Department."
   g. Drag the chart's selection handles so it fills the screen.
   h. Save your work.

2 Edit a chart and change the chart type.
  a. Change the value in cell B3 to 6.
  b. Select the chart by clicking on it.
  c. Click the Chart Type list arrow on the Chart toolbar.
  d. Click the 3-D Column Chart button in the list.
  e. Rotate the chart to move the data.
  f. Save your work.

3 Add a text annotation and an arrow to the current chart.
  a. Double-click the chart to put it in Edit mode.
  b. Create the text annotation "Need More Computers."
  c. Drag the text annotation about 1" above any of the Personnel bars.
  d. Click the Arrow button on the Draw toolbar.
  e. Click below the text annotation, drag down any one of the Personnel bars, then release the mouse button.
  f. Add arrows from the text annotation to each of the remaining Personnel bars.
  g. Open a second window so you can display the data in the new window and the chart in the original window.
  h. Close the second window.
  i. Save your work.

4 Enhance a chart.
  a. Make sure the chart is still in Edit mode, then click Insert on the menu bar, click Titles, click the Category (X) Axis check box, then click OK.
  b. Type "Department" in the selected text box below the x-axis, then click the Enter button on the formula bar.
  c. Click Insert on the menu bar, click Titles, select Value (Y) Series check box, then click OK.
  d. Type "Types of Software" in the selected text box to the left of the y-axis, then click the Enter button.
  e. Make any necessary adjustments to elements within the chart to make it look professional.
  f. Save your work.

5 Change the appearance of a chart.
  a. Make sure the chart is still in Edit mode.
  b. Click the Gridlines button on the Chart toolbar.
  c. Change the x- and y-axis font to Times New Roman.
  d. Save your work.

6 Move and resize a chart object.
  a. Make sure the chart is still in Edit mode.
  b. Click the legend to select it.
  c. Make the legend larger and wider by about ½".
  d. Move the legend below the charted data.
  e. Make any necessary adjustments to elements within the chart to make it look professional, such as moving the arrows so they point to the correct data series.
  f. Save your work.

7 Preview and print a chart.
  a. Make sure the chart is still in Edit mode, then click the Print Preview button on the Standard toolbar.
  b. Center the chart on the page and change the paper orientation to landscape.
  c. Click Print in the Print Preview window.
  d. Save your work, close the workbook, then exit Excel.

INDEPENDENT
CHALLENGE 1

You are the operations manager for the Springfield Recycling Center. The Marketing Department wants you to create charts for a brochure to advertise a new curbside recycling program. The data provided contains percentages of collected recycled goods. You need to create charts that show:

- How much of each type of recycled material Springfield collected in 1994 and what percentage each type represents. The center collects paper, plastics, and glass from business and residential customers.
- The yearly increases in the total amounts of recycled materials the center has collected since its inception three years ago. Springfield has experienced a 30% annual increase in collections.

To complete this independent challenge:

1 Prepare a worksheet plan that states your goal and identifies the formulas for any calculations.

2 Sketch a sample worksheet on a piece of paper describing how you will create the charts. Which type of chart is best suited for the information you need to display? What kind of chart enhancements will be necessary? Will a 3-D effect make your chart easier to understand?

3 Open the workbook XL 4-2 on your Student Disk, then save it as Recycling Center to the My Excel Files folder.

4 Add a column that calculates the 30% increase in annual collections.

5 Create at least six different charts to show the distribution of the different types of recycled goods, as well as the distribution by customer type. Use the ChartWizard to switch the way data is plotted (columns vs. rows and vice versa) and come up with additional charts.

6 After creating the charts, make the appropriate enhancements. Include chart titles, legends, and axes titles.

7 Before printing, preview the file so you know what the charts will look like. Adjust any items as needed.

8 Save your work. Print the charts, then print the entire worksheet. Close the file.

9 Submit your worksheet plan, preliminary sketches, and the final worksheet printouts.

INDEPENDENT
CHALLENGE 2

As an administrator with the U.S. Census Bureau, you are concerned with the population distribution by age and gender. You need to create charts that show:

- How the population is distributed, by age and gender
- How the population is distributed, by gender

AGE	MALE	FEMALE	AGE	MALE	FEMALE
65+	5%	7.5%	25-34	8.7%	8.7%
55-64	4%	4.5%	15-24	7.6%	7.3%
45-54	4.9%	5.2%	5-14	7.2%	6.9%
35-44	7.4%	7.6%	<5	3.9%	3.6%

To complete this independent challenge:

1 Prepare a worksheet plan that states your goal and identifies the formulas for any calculations.

2 Sketch a sample worksheet on a piece of paper describing how you will create the charts. Which type of charts are best suited for the information you need to display? What kind of chart enhancements will be necessary? Will a 3-D effect make your chart easier to understand?

3 Open a new workbook using the data above, and save it as Census Statistics to the My Excel Files folder on your Student Disk.

4 Create at least six different charts that show the population in its entirety, by gender, by age, and by both gender and age. Use the ChartWizard to switch the way data is plotted (columns vs. rows and vice versa) and come up with additional charts. Make sure your charts show the information requested above.

5 Add annotated text and arrows highlighting any data you feel is particularly important. Change colors to emphasize significant data.

6 Before printing, preview the file so you know what the charts will look like. Adjust any items as needed.

7 Print the charts. Save your work.

8 Submit your worksheet plan, preliminary sketches, and the final worksheet printouts.

INDEPENDENT
CHALLENGE 3

One of your responsibilities at the Nuts and Bolts hardware store is to re-create the company's records using Excel.

Another responsibility is to convince the current staff that Excel can make daily operations easier and more efficient. You've decided to create charts using the previous year's operating expenses. These charts will be used at the next monthly Accounting Department meeting.

Open the workbook XL 4-3 on your Student Disk, and save it as Expense Charts in the My Excel Files Folder.

To complete this independent challenge:

1 Decide which data in the worksheet should be charted. Sketch two sample charts. What type of charts are best suited for the information you need to display? What kind of chart enhancements will be necessary?

2 Create at least six different charts that show the distribution of expenses, either by quarter or expense type.

3 Add annotated text and arrows highlighting data.

4 In one chart, change the colors of data series, and in another chart, use black-and-white patterns only.

5 Before printing, preview the file so you know what the charts will look like. Adjust any items as needed.

6 Print the charts. Save your work.

7 Submit your sketches and the final worksheet printouts.

INDEPENDENT
CHALLENGE 4

The Chamber of Commerce is delighted with the work you've done on Excel. The Board of Directors wants to ask the city for additional advertising funds and has asked you to prepare charts that can be used in their presentation.

Open the workbook XL 4-4 on your Student Disk, and save it as Chamber Charts in the My Excel Files Folder. This file contains raw advertising data for the month of January.

To complete this independent challenge:

1 Using the raw data for January, calculate the distribution of advertising expenses in the range A16:B24.

2 Project the annual expenses if spending continues.

3 Decide what types of charts would be best suited for this type of data. Sketch two sample charts. What kind of chart enhancements will be necessary?

4 Create at least four different charts that show the distribution of advertising expenses. Show January expenses and projected values in at least two of the charts.

5 Add annotated text and arrows highlighting important data. Change the colors of data series if you wish.

6 Before printing, preview the file so you know what the charts will look like. Adjust any items as needed.

7 Print the charts. Save your work.

8 Submit your sketches and the final worksheet printouts.

VISUALWORKSHOP

Modify a worksheet using the skills you learned in this unit using Figure 4-23 for reference. Open the file XL 4-5 on your Student Disk, and save it as Quarterly Advertising Budget in the My Excel Files folder. Make your changes, preview and print your results, and submit your printout.

FIGURE 4-23

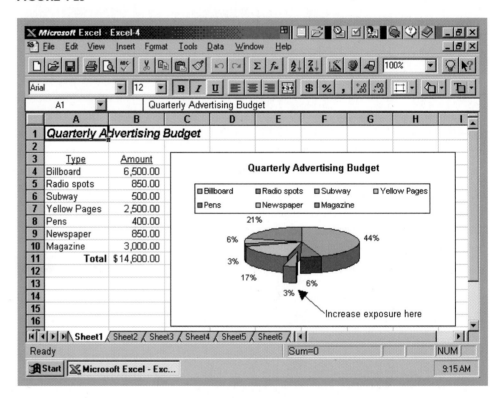

Glossary

Absolute reference   A cell reference that contains a dollar sign before the column letter and/or row number to indicate the absolute, or fixed, contents of specific cells. For example, the formula $A$1+$B$1 calculates only the sum of these specific cells.

Active cell   The current location of the cell pointer.

Address   The location of a specific cell or range expressed by the coordinates of column and row; for example, A1.

Alignment   The horizontal placement of cell contents; for example, left, center, or right.

Anchors   Cells listed in a range address. For example, in the formula =SUM(A1:A15), A1 and A15 are anchors.

Area chart   A line chart in which each area is given a solid color or pattern to emphasize the relationship between the pieces of charted information.

Argument   A value, range of cells, or text used in a macro or function. An argument is enclosed in parentheses; for example, =SUM(A1..B1).

Arithmetic operator   A symbol used in formulas, such as + or -.

Attribute   The styling features such as bold, italics, and underlining that can be applied to cell contents.

AutoCalculate box   The area in the status bar which displays the sum (or function of your choice) of the values in the selected range.

AutoComplete   A feature that automatically completes labels entered in adjoining cells in a column.

AutoFill   A feature that creates a series of text or numbers when a range is selected using the fill handle.

AutoFormat   Preset schemes which can be applied to instantly format a range. Excel comes with sixteen AutoFormats which include colors, fonts, and numeric formatting.

Background color   The color applied to the background of a cell.

Bar chart   The bar chart displays information as the series of (horizontal) bars.

Border   Edges of a selected area of a worksheet. Lines and color can be applied to borders.

Cancel button   The X in the formula bar, the Cancel button removes information from the formula bar and restores the previous cell entry.

Cascading menu   A subgroup of related commands that display beside a drop-down menu.

Cell   The intersection of a column and row.

Cell address   Unique location identified by intersecting column and row coordinates.

Cell pointer   A highlighted rectangle around a cell that indicates the active cell.

Cell reference   The address or name of a specific cell; cell references can be used in formulas and are relative or absolute.

Chart   A graphic representation of selected worksheet information. Types include 2-D and 3-D column, bar, pie, area, and line charts.

Chart title   The name assigned to a chart.

ChartWizard   A series of dialog boxes which helps create or modify a chart.

Check box   A square box in a dialog box that can be clicked to turn an option on or off.

Clear   A command used to erase a cell's contents, formatting, or both.

Clipboard   A temporary storage area for cut or copied items that are available for pasting.

Close   A command that puts a file away but keeps Excel open so that you can continue to work on other workbooks.

Column chart   The default chart type in Excel. The column chart displays information as a series of (vertical) columns.

Column selector button   The gray box containing the column letter above the column.

Confirm button   The check mark in the formula bar, the Confirm button is used to confirm an entry.

Control menu box   A box in the upper-left corner of a window used to resize or close a window.

Copy   A command that copies the selected information and places it on the Clipboard.

Cut   A command that removes the contents from a selected area of a worksheet and places them on the Clipboard.

Data marker   Visible representation of a data point, such as a bar or pie slice.

Data point   Individual piece of data plotted in a chart.

Data series   The selected range in a worksheet that Excel converts into a graphic and displays as a chart.

Delete   A command that removes cell contents from a worksheet.

Delete records   A command that removes records from a list.

Dialog box   A window that displays when you choose a command whose name is followed by an ellipsis (...). A dialog box allows you to make selections that determine how the command affects the selected area.

Drop-down menu   A group of related commands located under a single word on the menu bar. For example, basic commands (New, Open, Save, Close, and Print) are grouped on the File menu.

Dummy column/row   Blank column or row included at the end of a range which enables a formula to adjust when columns or rows are added or deleted.

Edit   A change made to the contents of a cell or worksheet.

Electronic spreadsheet   A computer program that performs calculations on data and organizes information. A spreadsheet is divided into columns and rows, which form individual cells.

Ellipsis   A series of dots (...) indicating that more choices are available through dialog boxes.

Exploding pie slice   A slice of a pie chart which has been pulled away from a pie to add emphasis.

Fill Down   A command that duplicates the contents of the selected cells in the range selected below the cell pointer.

Fill handle   Small square in the lower-right corner of the active cell used to copy cell contents.

Fill Right   A command that duplicates the contents of the selected cells in the range selected to the right of the cell pointer.

Find   A command used to locate information the user specifies.

Find & Replace   A command used to find one set of criteria and replace it with new information.

Floating toolbar   A toolbar within its own window; not anchored along an edge of the worksheet.

Folder   A section of a disk used to store workbooks, much like a folder in a file cabinet.

Font   The typeface used to display information in cells.

Format   The appearance of text and numbers, including color, font, attributes, and worksheet defaults. See also number format.

Formula   A set of instructions that you enter in a cell to perform numeric calculations (adding, multiplying, averaging, etc.); for example, +A1+B1.

Formula bar   The area below the menu bar and above the Excel workspace where you enter and edit data in a worksheet cell. The formula bar becomes active when you start typing or editing cell data. The formula bar includes an Enter button and a Cancel button.

Freeze   The process of making columns or rows visible.

Function   A special predefined formula that provides a shortcut for commonly used calculations; for example, AVERAGE.

Function Wizard   A series of dialog boxes that lists and describes all Excel functions and assists the user in function creation.

Gridlines   Horizontal and/or vertical lines within a chart which makes the chart easier to read.

Input   Information which produces desired results in a worksheet.

Insertion point   Blinking I-beam which appears in the formula bar during entry and editing.

Label   Descriptive text or other information that identify the rows and columns of a worksheet. Labels are not included in calculations.

Label prefix   A character that identifies an entry as a label and controls the way it is displayed in the cell.

Landscape orientation   Printing on a page whose dimensions are 11" (horizontally) by 8½" (vertically).

Launch   To open a software program so you can use it.

Legend   A key explaining the information represented by colors or patterns in a chart.

Line chart   A graph of data that is mapped by a series of lines. Line charts show changes in data or categories of data over time and can be used to document trends.

Menu bar   The area under the title bar on a window. The menu bar provides access to most of the application's commands.

Mode indicator A box located at the lower-left corner of the status bar that informs you of the program's status. For example, when Excel is performing a task, the work "Wait" displays.

Mouse pointer A symbol that indicates the current location of the mouse on the desktop. The mouse pointer changes shapes at times; for example, when you insert data, select a range, position a chart, change the size of a window, or select a topic in Help.

Name box The left-most area in the formula bar that shows the name or address of the area currently selected. For example, A1 refers to cell A1 of the current worksheet.

Number format A format applied to values to express numeric concepts, such as currency, date, and percent.

Object A chart or graphic image which can be moved and resized and contains handles when selected.

Open A command that retrieves a workbook from a disk and displays it on the screen.

Order of precedence The order in which Excel calculates parts of a formula: (1) exponents, (2) multiplication and division, and (3) addition and subtraction.

Output The end result of a worksheet.

Pane A column or row which always remains visible.

Paste A command that moves information on the Clipboard to a new location. Excel pastes the formulas, rather than the result unless the Paste Special command is used.

Paste Special A command that enables you to paste formulas as values, styles, or cell contents.

Pie chart A circular chart that displays data as slices of pie. A pie chart is useful for showing the relationship of parts to a whole; pie slices can be extracted for emphasis.

Point A unit of measure used for fonts and row height. One inch equals 72 points.

Print Preview window A window that displays a reduced view of area to be printed.

Program Software, such as Excel or Word, that enables you to perform a certain type of task, such as data calculations or word processing.

Program Manager The main control program of Windows. All Windows applications are started from the Program Manager.

Program Menu The Windows 95 Start menu that lists all the available programs on your computer.

Radio button A circle in a dialog box that can be clicked when only one option can be chosen.

Random Access Memory (RAM) A temporary storage area in a computer that is erased each time the computer is turned off or whenever there is a fluctuation in power. When a program is launched, it is loaded into RAM so you can work with that program.

Range A selected group of adjacent cells.

Range format A format applied to a selected range in a worksheet.

Range name A name applied to a selected range in a worksheet.

Relative cell reference Used to indicate a relative position in the worksheet. This allows you to copy and move formulas from one area to another of the same dimensions. Excel automatically changes the column and row numbers to reflect the new position.

Row height The vertical dimension of a cell.

Row selector button The gray box containing the row number to the left of the row.

Save A command used to save incremental changes to a workbook.

Save As A command used to create a duplicate of the current workbook.

Scroll bars Bars that display on the right and bottom borders of the worksheet window that give you access to information not currently visible in the current worksheet as well as others in the workbook.

Selection handles Small boxes appearing along the corners and sides of charts and graphic images which are used for moving and resizing.

Series of labels Pre-programmed series, such as days of the week and months of the year. Formed by typing the first word of the series, then dragging the fill handle to the desired cell.

Sheet A term used for worksheet.

Sheet tab scrolling buttons Enable you to move among sheets within a workbook.

Spell check A command that attempts to match all text in a worksheet with the words in the Excel dictionary.

Status bar The bar near the bottom of the screen that provides information about the tasks Excel is performing or about any current selections.

Start To open a software program so you can use it.

Start button   The rectangular button at the left end of the taskbar which displays the Windows 95 menus.

Taskbar   The gray bar, usually at the bottom of the screen, containing the Start button, as well as program buttons for all programs currently running.

Text annotations   Labels added to a chart to draw attention to a particular area.

Text color   The color applied to the text within a cell.

Title bar   The bar at the top of the window that displays the name given a workbook when it is saved and named.

Toggle button   A button that can be clicked to turn an option on. Clicking again turns the option off.

Tool   A picture on a toolbar that represents a shortcut for performing an Excel task. For example, you can click the Save tool to save a file.

Toolbar   An area within the Excel screen which contains tools. Toolbars can be docked against a worksheet edge or can float.

ToolTip   Description of a tool, which appears in a toolbar, under the tool.

Values   Numbers, formulas, or functions used in calculations.

What-if analysis   Decision-making feature in which data is changed and automatically recalculated.

Window   A framed area of a screen. Each worksheet occupies a window.

Workbook   A collection of related worksheets contained within a single file.

Worksheet   An electronic spreadsheet containing 256 columns by 16,384 rows.

Worksheet tab   A description at the bottom of each worksheet that identified it in a workbook. In an open workbook, move to a worksheet by clicking its tab.

X-axis   The horizontal line in a chart.

X-axis label   A label describing the x-axis of a chart.

Y-axis   The vertical line in a chart.

Y-axis label   A label describing the y-axis of a chart.

Zoom   Enables you to focus on a larger or smaller part of the worksheet in print preview.

Index